THE SAL

Text by

CHRISTINE MAXA

Photographs by

DAVID A. JAMES

ISBN:	978-0-9785824-3-2
TEXT:	Christine Maxa - © 2009. All rights reserved
PHOTOGRAPHY:	David A. James - © 2009. All rights reserved
BOOK & DESIGN:	Jamax Publishers Press - © 2009. All rights reserved
EDITOR:	Robert J. Early
COPY EDITOR:	Jim Veideffer
PUBLISHER:	Graham County Chamber of Commerce
	1111 Thatcher Boulevard
	Safford, Arizona 85546 U.S.A.
	Sheldon Miller - Executive Director
PRODUCTION & PRE-PRESS:	Jamax Publishers Press, Kirkland, Arizona U.S.A.
	Christine Maxa - Publisher
	David James - Production Manager
MAPS:	National Geographic Topo! ® 1:24,000 (2006)
PRINTED IN:	China
	H & Y Printing Company, Hong Kong
TYPESETTING:	*Typeset* in Myriad Pro® by Jamax Enterprises Incorported, Kirkland, Arizona U.S.A.

DISTRIBUTED BY: *Jamax Publishers Press, Kirkland, Arizona U.S.A.*

LIBRARY OF CONGRESS CATALOGING-IN-PUBLICATION DATA

Maxa, Christine.
The Salsa Trail
Photography by David A. James (1943-)
Includes bibliographic references (v.1, p.) and index
ISBN: 978-0-97858224-3-2
1. Cookery, salsa. - 2. Cookery, guidebook. - 3. Tourism, culinary guidebook. - 4. Arizona, guidebooks. - I. title.

2009921061

First Edition 2009 - This is a Jamax Outdoor Guidebook.

Special Disclaimer - Please Note:

Recipes using raw or lightly cooked eggs should be avoided by infants, the elderly, pregnant women, convalescents and persons suffering from illness. Consumption of peanuts should be avoided by pregnant and breast-feeding women. Consumption of chile peppers by infants and young children should be avoided. Risk is always a factor in backcountry and mountain travel. Many of the outdoor activities described in this book can be dangerous, especially during adverse or unpredictable weather or when unforeseen events or conditions create a hazardous situation. The author and publisher disclaim any liability for injury or other damage caused by backcountry and mountain travel, food selection and preparation, or any other activity described in this book.

Previous page - Author's hiking hat hangs over a rista from the San Simon Chile Company - Photograph by D. James

It all started in the valley of the Puebla Viejo

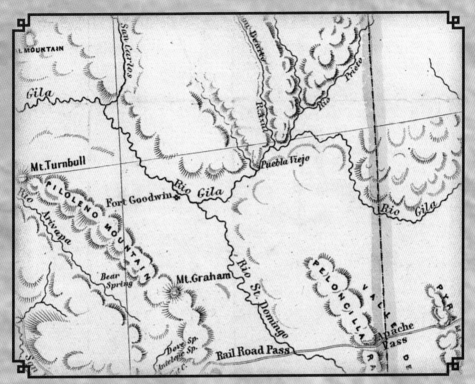

*along a strip of fertile land that bordered Arizona's
Gila River and whose year-round waters nourished the
first Indian and Spanish settlers of Arizona. Agricul-
ture blossomed here and, with it, the simple foods of the
earth that developed into those dishes so well known to
Mexican and Spanish palates. Little of the countryside
is changed, much has improved, and the beauty remains.
These are the roots of the Salsa Trail. The food, the
land and the people, that's what this book is all about.*

Graham County Chamber of Commerce

Contents

Soups, Sauces & Marinades

Side Dishes

Desserts

Food, Destinations & Activities

Food

Activities

Backcountry Spots

Safford Geothermal Area   144

Walking Tours & Scenic Drives

Accommodations

Everything you see in this book is a product of real Arizona – the food, the scenery, the people. In an effort to preserve the simple, but full, life along Arizona's Salsa Trail, everything was recorded in the moment. The food was photographed just as it came from each restaurant's kitchen onto the table in their dining area. No studio kitchens, food dressers or artificial products were employed to make these images. What you see in this book is what you get, slow-food freshly made and very delicious. In short, a foodie's delight!

You will find many little known facts about a culture-packed, out-of-the-way part of Arizona. This incredibly beautiful landscape holds many rare and wonderful sights – the gentle greening of a gnarly volcanic landscape in the spring, a summertime glance at 200-foot-high Ash Creek Falls, the gently rolling foothills strawed golden by the first fall frost, thousands of sandhill cranes rising to meet the winter morning sun. If you enjoy reading this book as much as we did creating it, then our job is well done.

Christine and David.

ACKNOWLEDGEMENTS

Whatever request we presented to Sheldon Miller, executive director of the Graham County Chamber of Commerce, he always answered: "Your demand, our command." His assistant, Marie Freestone, had enthusiasm and kindness that always made communications with her a pleasure. Bill Civish, chairman of the Graham County Chamber of Commerce Tourism Committee gave invaluable experience.

We especially want to express our deep appreciation for the venues along Arizona's Salsa Trail for their patience as we took pictures and interviewed them. We apologize for any excessive drooling over their delicious food and thank them for allowing us to indulge on the spot and/or sending us away with generous care packages of yummies.

We also send a special thanks to:

The team at Eurofresh Farms. Their generosity in time, talent and wonderful tomatoes (they really are the best) was over the top.
John Ratje, from the University of Arizona and site manager of the Large Binocular Telescope project atop Mt. Graham (it really is out of this world).

Mel Jones, with the Graham County Historical Society, and Don Lunt from the Greenlee County Historical Society, who had avid listeners as they expounded tirelessly about the history of their communities in really fascinating detail.

Freeport MacMoRan Copper & Gold, which gave us a tour of its Morenci Mine (it really is big).

We also thank the staff at *Eastern Arizona College,* especially *Todd Haynie,* director, marketing and public relations; *Linda Blan,* anthropology faculty; and *David Morris,* division chair, science astronomy/geology faculty for their assistance with the culture and geology along Arizona's Salsa Trail; the innkeepers of the historic B&Bs along Arizona's Salsa Trail (*Chris and Deborah Gibbs* of the *Olney House, Deborah Mendelsohn* owner of the *Simpson Hotel* and *June Palmer* of the *Potter House*), who were a wealth of information and assistance; and the men and women in the *United States Department of Interior, Bureau of Land Management* for their professionalism, their particular knowledge of the land and their invaluable tidbits of information.

Photo Credits - Mark Downey

P. 12 center. P. 14 upper right. P. 17 upper left & middle. P. 20 bottom. P. 22 top. P. 24 center & inserts on panorama. P. 25 top. P. 26 center. P. 29 insert at bottom. P. 32. P. 37 top. P. 38. P. 40 bottom. P. 41. P. 115 bottom. P. 116 bottom. P. 165 middle & bottom.

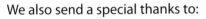

Photo above: From left, Laura Whelton, Marie Freestone and JoAn Surber, the ladies behind Señor Salsa

The Making of the Award-winning Arizona's Salsa Trail

Traditionally, Arizona history features The Four Cs – Copper, Cattle, Cotton and Citrus – as integral to the state's prosperity. A fifth, Climate, sometimes gets unofficially added to the list. Señor Salsa, the main character in this book, insists Arizona add a sixth: Chile Peppers.

In an attempt to promote this addition of the chile pepper, Señor Salsa actually showed up at the Graham County Chamber of Commerce one day. Sheldon Miller, executive director of the Graham County Chamber of Commerce tells the real story….

"We-e-e-e-l-l-l," Miller began in his matter-of-fact, singsong way, "culinary tourism started to become a big deal, and we took a look at the restaurants we had. They were all regional and rooted in Mexican culture."

 Miller's Graham County compadre in tourism, Bill Civish, saw the light. As a practicing foodie, Civish understood how soulfully satisfying good, home-made Mexican food can be.

"We grabbed a bit of salsa from each restaurant," Miller continued, "bought some chips from Mi Casa Tortilla Factory and went to the director's office at the Arizona Office of Tourism with bowls, tablecloth and curiosity.

"We didn't necessarily want to sell the idea of Arizona's Salsa Trail," Miller admitted. "We went to see if the big-city state agency even knew we existed."

Not located on "the way to" any tourist attraction and far enough away from the sizeable cities of Arizona, Señor Salsa's stomping grounds often get left off the tourism map. Though the Arizona Office of Tourism staff never actually acknowledged it knew what direction Arizona's Salsa Trail committee came from, the idea of Arizona's Salsa Trail did impress them. They also, Señor Salsa disclosed, devoured the yummy salsa and chips. He claimed he thought he saw one person actually lick the bowls clean.

Not only did Arizona's Salsa Trail impress the state tourism director, she realized Graham County had itself a piece of bona fide culinary tourism without even trying. Not polished and precise like some resort restaurants gleaming with Mobil- and AAA-appointed stars and diamonds – it was happening as a matter of fact. Diners may as well be sitting in a familia kitchen when they sit down at some of the restaurants on Arizona's Salsa Trail.

"We didn't know what we had," Miller mused. "It was normal to us. We went home and thought we better do something about this."

Promoting Arizona's Salsa Trail did not come easy. First, never had a group of small restaurants worked together to promote a single cause that wasn't really important to them to begin with. Generally, most small establishments have a sole interest in keeping their doors open. These restaurants had been open for years and enjoyed a regular clientele. Why fix things if they weren't broken?

Next, most restaurateurs either wouldn't, or couldn't, share recipes because of secrecy or no standardization (measuring by sight and sense rather than using precision devices). This did not daunt Arizona's Salsa Trail committee, who gathered recipes from all points along the path.

Food may be the fastest way to the heart, but Graham County Chamber of Commerce also knew it had some pretty interesting things going on that visitors might not find anywhere else in the state – world-class birding on the Lower Sonoran Desert floor and sub-alpine meadows; sky island hiking and historic scenic drives, hot springs and snow-capped mountains, poetic starry night skies and the specialized telescopes peering into them, exclusive fire agate fields and mega-mines. Arizona's Salsa Trail had the best of many worlds.

What could be more perfect? Good, homemade and real Mexican food; unique natural wonders; creature comforts; environmental interests, scenic beauty and outdoor challenges. Arizona's Salsa Trail became all things to all people. And it happened so naturally. So naturally the good people who live along Arizona's Salsa Trail expect you will have a special, eventful and beneficial time.

Epilogue

The Arizona Office of Tourism staff knew all along that the towns on Arizona's Salsa Trail existed. It not only knew, but it memorialized its support for those off-the-map places. Arizona Office of Tourism presented Graham County Chamber of Commerce the Innovative Promotions award at the 2008 Governor's Conference on Tourism for Arizona's Salsa Trail.

Photo opposite page: Bill Civish with his chile verde dish and the Governor's Award for Innovative Promotion

9

Arizona's Salsa Trail Venues

The non-native history of the southern half of Arizona often begins with the Hispanic culture. In eastern Arizona, the migration started with Francisco Vásquez de Coronado when he led an entourage northward from just outside Mexico City in the 16th century to New Mexico, and then eventually points northeastward.

When Anglo settlers first came to the Upper Gila Valley in the mid-1870s, several Hispanic families had already established farms near the confluence of the San Francisco and Gila rivers. Most of the Mexican settlers migrated from New Mexico and Sonora and Chihuahua, Mexico. Lorenzo Sanchez drew some of the first irrigation waters from the Rio del Nombre de Jesus, or Gila River, once the boundary line between Mexico and the United States before the Treaty of Guadalupe Hidalgo in 1848.

The Gila and San Francisco rivers always drew farmers to its side, from native peoples to Hispanic, then Mormon, settlers.

Later, Hispanic immigrants traveled into the United States to escape the social inequities that roiled before the Mexican Revolution. They came via routes trod by native peoples and later traveled by so many explorers and great names in history: Geronimo, de Anza, de Niza, and Coronado; some of which are now part of The Old West Highway or US 70.

Hispanics from mineral-rich Sonora and Chihuahua, Mexico had centuries of ranchers' and prospectors' blood in their veins and followed the big strikes around Arizona to work in the mines or provide food and other necessities to the miners.

Wherever these Mexican immigrants settled, so came their culture. They built adobe homes, honored their spiritual traditions and ate foods familiar to their south-of-the-border homes. The foods originally differed from what's served in many Mexican restaurants today – a combination of northern Mexico and Texas cowboy called Tex-Mex. Oh, they had their beloved tortilla and chile peppers, but no goopy cheese, less meat, different spices and little of the deep-frying so common to Tex-Mex.

In the 1970s, Tex-Mex became vogue. Once the trend hit Paris, the rest of the world was not far behind. Even Bangkok and the Middle East indulged. Señor Salsa, you might say, has been around the block a few times.

What was newfangled for the rest of the world was a way of life back here along Arizona's Salsa Trail. The following pages feature all the official restaurants and venues that comprise Arizona's Salsa Trail, and each one displays a sign (right) signifying it is an official venue along the Trail. Every one of them has a history, some more than a half-century. And every one of them has a following they're proud to live up to. This makes the geo-traveler's axiom, Go where the locals go, a difficult piece of advice to follow here along Arizona's Salsa Trail. With that in mind, Señor Salsa recommends you follow another axiom, When in Rome, do as the Romans do. Just join the locals and try them all.

Photos opposite page: From top, (1) Duncan area farmer, (2) cattle along US 70, (3) abandoned adit near Clifton **This page:** *(1) Official Salsa trail sign (2) Three young wine aficionados at Coronado Vineyards*

El Coronado

(928) 428-7755 409 Main St.
Safford (closed Tues)

Coronado means crowned. For Mary Coronado, owner and chef of El Coronado family restaurant, the name fits. Her food has won awards, gotten national press, and earned local admiration.

Her story starts back in 1983 when a restaurateur approached Coronado with, "I hear you like to cook" and an offer to hire her. Coronado who always entertained at home and loved her kitchen, agreed to try it. And she liked it. Within months she opened El Coronado, which became not just a place to eat, but to be.

Go in the morning, around 9:30, and you'll find the town fathers gathered around the back table, running the town, they joke, from their appointed spot. Later, after lunch, a handful of locals line up along the counter for their daily cup o' Joe.

The meeting place turns eating place with classic Mexican and signature dishes like Steak Picado and Huevos Rancheros. The latter got notable mention in a *U.S. News & World Report* article as the best in the West. What makes the *huevos* so special? Coronado ladles her award-winning salsa over them. The secret to this salsa is in the spices.

"Everyone has tomatoes, chilies, and onions in their salsa," Coronado explained. "It's the combination of spices I use that makes mine so good."

Good enough to win two first-place awards – *The People's Choice and the Judges' Choice* – at *Graham County's 2007 Salsa Festival*. Coronado says the salsa contest was a hallmark of her career "because the competition was stiff." El Coronado serves up *four gallons* of this salsa a day. Diners will go through several bottles of it in one sitting. For some, this is a daily habit.

After 25 years in the El Coronado kitchen, Coronado prepares not only the salsa, but the green chili meat (her personal favorite), red chili meat, enchilada sauces, guacamole, and pumpkin empanadas (they're so special because they're made with anise). Still, she continues to make a new discovery now and again. A local farmer recently brought her a bag of beans to sample. As she describes how tasty the beans cooked up, her eyes beam and her hands accentuate her surprise find.

"They're beautiful," she gushed about the *habas* as only a bona fide foodie would. "They're fresh, real soft, and just cook up different. I didn't think beans could taste this good."

Besides beautiful beans, trophy salsa and famous *huevos,* El Coronado serves desserts by Della. Working in the restaurant since she was six years old, Coronado's daughter Della can make all the dishes on the menu. Desserts, however, are her calling; and the strawberry and chocolate cakes the most popular – *la coronas de El Coronado's creaciones.*

Photos opposite page: From top, (1) Mary Coronado (2) El Coronado's retro-interior (3) El Coronado street entrance **This page:** *(1) Panorama of Mary's creative kitchen (2) Mary with her daughters (3) Mary' steak picado and Della's famous strawberry cake*

CHALO'S

(928-348-9889 / 928-348-9941) 611 South Sixth Avenue, Safford

When Salustia Reynoso started her restaurant, El Rey, in 1936, Arizona's lineage of Mexican food restaurants was never quite the same. Little did she know a family tree of restaurants would sprout in points around the Southwest, from El Rey in Globe to Los Compadres in Phoenix to Chalo's here in Safford, and then several in Miami, Thatcher, the Mogollon Rim and New Mexico in between. All serve food made with the same recipes Salustia created. Chalo's in Safford, named for Salustia's son, Gonzalo (nicknamed Chalo), opened in 1994 by Lisa Jones, Chalo's daughter. Chalo, now 72, still comes by now and again and heads right for the kitchen to do some cooking when he visits.

"The family calls it The Great Inheritance," explained Jones. "People don't know how connected the restaurants are. They are a family experience."

Everything is done by hand at Chalo's, Jones said. For instance, rather than frying pre-made and frozen chile rellenos, Chalo's whips eggs like a meringue then rolls fresh peppers hand-stuffed with cheese (more than 200 each week) in the coating. The ambrosial result has a texture akin to velvet. The soups for their sauces are made from scratch and tamales are still prepared by hand, right in the kitchen. Even the Margaritas get made from scratch, with fresh lime juice and a choice of 20 different tequilas. Their signature fajita dishes are a fiesta of food.

Fare like this rarely gets past the famous, and the Reynoso restaurants have seen their share. Former Senator Dennis DeConcini flew the family to Washington, D.C. to make a dinner. Former Department of the Interior Secretary Gale Norton and Congressman Rick Renzi have shown up in this Chalo's, as well as hard rock star, Ted Nugent.

The Reynosos know they have a good thing. With a reputation for some of the best green chile, indulging in labor-intensive items like chile rellenos and tamales and filling quart containers of salsa and enchilada sauce to go, they are not quick to share their savory secrets.

Photos this page: From top, (1) Bean Burrito Enchilada style, (2) two of Chalo's many servers (3) Chalo's Chef and his busy kitchen

Chile rellenos combination plate –
The Chalo's name is famous across the nation.

Jones still goes into her secret space – her laboratory – to mix spices. She puts them into unlabeled plastic bags and tells the chef which one is used for what dish. No one else knows, except Chalo (and Salustia), the secret behind the good food.

BUSH & SHURTZ

(928-485-0679) 232 E. 300 South Old Highway, Pima

You have to veer a bit off the beaten path of the Old West Highway to find this local favorite located in an icehouse built in 1905. In the 1930s, Charlie Bush opened a hardware store in the building with a partner and they named it after themselves. Margie and Eddie Robinson started the restaurant in 1999 and kept the name Bush & Shurtz "because everyone knew where it was," Margie explained.

In a place where the clock has a face that reads "Who Cares?" above a jumble of numbers, you can imagine the sense of humor that prevails. You may have to take the wall art and local banter with a few grains of salt, but the food is down-home simple but good.

The favorites here are the burgers, enchiladas, salsa and fried ice cream. Bush & Shurtz serves one of the best hamburgers in the Gila Valley at one of the best prices ($4.25 for the Bushy Burger and $3.25 for the Shurtz Burger). The prices were inspired by a customer who said to Margie one day, "I've got four dollars, and I'm hungry."

"The hamburger is grill-made," said Eddie, who cooks all the food, "so it's not greasy. There's a trick to grilling. We don't press the juice out or poke it with a fork."

The salsa, which took the Robinsons two years to perfect, has nine different ingredients. They used customer feedback to fine-tune the recipe that, customers claim, does not cause heartburn.

"I have people offer me money for the recipe," Eddie said about the salsa. "Or they say, 'I won't tell Margie if you give me the recipe.'"

Besides some good food, you can get an earful of gen-u-ine farmer banter when the Farmer's

Club comes for their lunch. As dependable as the sun rising and setting, the group of Gila Valley farmers meets at 1 p.m. every day the restaurant is open. They even get their own table at the front of the restaurant. Every topic at their table

This Section Reserved For
The BUSH & SHURTZ
FARMERS CLUB
1 PM To 3 PM DAILY

is fair game, nothing is sacred and advice is rife.

The Robinsons figure Bush & Shurtz has remained the town meeting place since its hardware store days because they basically give their customers what they want. People just have to walk through the door and Margie knows what they want. Some come in and merely signal with two fingers. This, being interpreted, means two cheese enchiladas.

"We're not fancy," Margie explained, "but if you feel like dancing, go right ahead. We just treat everybody like family."

*Photos opposite page: From top, (1) owner Margie Robinson (2) Bush & Shurtz, (3) Eddie Robinson at the grill, (4) inside the kitchen **This page:** (1) Farmer's Club gathering, (2) Farmer's Club reserved sign, (3) friendly enthusiasm greets all visitors (4) Cheese enchilada plate.*

Along the Salsa Trail - Real Arizona

La Casita Café

(928-428-1882) 3338 W. Main Street, Thatcher

Hope, desire and Salustia Reynoso's recipes created La Casita in 1947 – not this La Casita, but the one in Globe, Arizona. Salustia, revered for her recipes, is practically the patron saint of Mexican food restaurants in these parts. Her recipes are not only used in the Globe restaurant, but also in this one at Thatcher.

"She was my mother-in-law's mother," said Lorraine Villalobos about Salustia.

Lorraine and her husband, Ray, opened the Thatcher La Casita restaurant in 1998. She manages and works the dining room, and he cooks the food. You'd never guess Ray didn't know a thing about cooking when he started. He wasn't even sure he could pull it off, but he's done his grandmother proud.

"He loves cooking," Lorraine said. "I told him he has his grandmother's spirit."

Every day the restaurant door opens, Ray gets into the kitchen at 4 a.m. to start his Salsa Trail magic. He cooks all the sauces (enchilada, green chile and red chile), beans, rice, guacamole, salsas and machaca.

When the restaurant opens for lunch at 11 a.m., diners pile in, filling up just about every table. But Ray won't generally finish his stint in the kitchen until 2 p.m. After he finishes cooking, he has himself a red chile beef and beans burro with butter on top. Every day.

Photos this page: From top, (1) La Casita's History (2) La Casita's Dish-Out Javier Avane, (3) Preparation of a Chimichanga (3) (l) machaca and (r) sopaipillas

Diners generally know what they want here at La Casita because, like Ray, the menu never changes. They do wonder, however, just what Ray puts into his mild salsa. People say it has a particular taste akin to cinnamon, but Lorraine said it isn't. She also said Ray won't budge in divulging the mystery ingredient. She will say the hot salsa has roasted peppers, roasted tomatoes and onion. Also, the green chile has both pork and beef in it; the machaca is juicy, and not dry; and the sopaipillas, her favorite, are light little pillows of air for which they are named. But that's about all. The kitchen belongs to Ray, and that's that.

"I'm so proud of Ray," Lorraine said. "People say, because the food's so good, 'Can we take him home with us?' I tell them, 'No!'"

Which is smart, because Ray doesn't do any of the cooking at home. That's where Lorraine takes over, except for barbecues.

"Even the barbecue is special," Lorraine said. "I don't know what he does, but it is good."

Green Chile Cheese Crisp
with house salsas

La Paloma
(928 428-2094) 5185 Clifton Street, Solomon

La Paloma has always been a favorite restaurant in the Valley. That's the main reason why owner, Tom Claridge, bought it.

"I always liked this restaurant," Claridge recalled the story of how he came to purchase the venue. "It was my favorite in the Valley. One day when I came in for a meal the former owner asked since I liked it so much, did I want to buy it? I thought he was kidding at first. But he wasn't, and I said, 'yes.'"

The restaurant has the same recipes and the same good food since the day it opened as Shorty's Café a half-century ago. It was always crowded when Shorty owned it, and the crowds didn't stop when Pat Hernandez bought it around 40 years ago and changed its name to La Paloma.

Four owners later, the crowds and name are not the only thing that has remained the same. It also has the same chefs. Chefs Carmen and Fernando come with the deal every time the restaurant changes hands. And they still cook upon the same cast iron and porcelain stove that Shorty used.

Fernando comes in each morning at 6:30 to get the kitchen going. Nicknamed the Sauce Master, he cooks up the green and red chile sauces, as well as the pinto beans. The red chile sauce, a restaurant trademark, has a secret blend of spices, which includes freshly ground red chile peppers. Carmen makes the other restaurant trademark, Chili Rellenos.

"The recipe is 40 years old," Carmen said as she prepared a batch for the evening dinner crowd. "I can tell you what goes in, but not how much. I always cook like that – inspiration and intuition. I don't measure. I just put everything together."

Carmen, the undisputed Queen of the Kitchen, also introduced Beef Empanadas on the menu, a recipe she learned from a friend in Mexico containing *masadina* (corn dough), green chile and onion. A ladle-full of red sauce transforms it into ambrosia. Anything made with Fernando's red sauce is a customer favorite, especially the enchiladas. Some people travel for hours to feast on a plate of the restaurant's enchiladas.

"The distinctive flavor of the sauces comes from Fernando's technique," explained Claridge. "Customers who have been coming here for years come in and know what they want. Often they'll call and just say, 'This is 'So-and-So'. I'll be there in five minutes'. We know exactly what they want, and the meal's practically ready and waiting for them when they get here."

Don't stop at the Enchiladas, however. Anything made by the Sauce Master and the Queen of the Kitchen is a royal treat.

Photos opposite page: From top, (1) Shorty's original stove, (2) Fernando, the sauce master, (3) from left; Carmen and La Paloma servers. This page: fried ice-cream (inset) and chile relleno and empanada plate

Manor House & Rock N' Horse Saloon
(928-428-7148) 415 E. US 70, Safford

"Presentation is everything," said Mary Lou Krieg, the Manor House's owner and chef as she watched her assistant, Tiffany Newton, place a taco and fan it out to complete the restaurant's signature combination plate.

While she perfected the placement of the beef taco, two enchiladas, rice and beans on the plate, Krieg said she creates all the recipes on the menu. Mostly, they come from her more than 30 years of experience as a chef. The self-proclaimed "hotel brat" has been in the business all her life. But she said she also listens to her staff, which relays concepts and requests from customers.

The Chicken Fried Steak is big, and the restaurant sells a lot of prime rib. But Krieg currently is gushing about her latest creation—Alaskan Wild Salmon with a Jack Daniels sauce. And then there's the Tuscan Chicken pasta dish with garlic butter cheese biscuits. Not everything on Arizona's Salsa Trail is salsa and Mexican.

"We've got it all," Krieg said. "You can bring in a party of eight, and it's all cooked fresh."

Pasties, a mixture of meat and vegetables in a crust (like a hand-held pot pie),

Along the Salsa Trail - Real Arizona

are a favorite with Krieg's granddaughters. The girls file into the restaurant after school to have a snack and visit with their grandparents. Krieg, who owns Freighter's Restaurant at Sault Ste. Marie, Michigan, imported the pasties idea from a 150-year-old tradition in Upper Michigan where iron and copper miners brought them to work. The local miners here in the desert like to take them for an on-site lunch and pick up an order on the way to work. The meat- and vegetable-filled turnovers (pork and beef with rutabagas, carrots, onion and special seasoning) can be a labor of love.

"We get a little miffed at the dough, sometimes," Krieg admitted. "If the temperature of the lard's not right or the humidity is too high, it makes a difference in the dough."

But this doesn't mean Señor Salsa's favorite fare served in places that feel like home takes a back seat to the Manor House's fine dining.

"For a fine dining restaurant," Krieg explained, "we're as casual as you can get. Plus, I won the green chile contest at the first *SalsaFest*. And I'm a gringa."

*Photo opposite page: Chef and owner Mary Lou Krieg (center, front) and her staff **Above:** Wild Salmon with Jack Daniels sauce **Below:** panorama of Krieg's kitchen*

Mi Casa Tortilla Factory

(928-428-7915) 621 Seventh Avenue, Safford

"I was ready to retire," reflected Manuel Bertoldo, owner of the freshest tortilla factory this side of the Gila River. "Then I saw an ad in the newspaper to buy this tortilla factory. I bought it on April 1, 1990 and I'm still working."

After Bertoldo offered a package of his flour tortillas to a couple, he declared, "I'm not doing you any favors. Everyone says the tortillas are so good. People drive from Phoenix and Tucson to buy them."

The reason? First, they're fresh. Bertoldo buys the corn, cooks it and then mills it. Second, he never adds preservatives, which alter the taste of foods. The result produces a home taste, not home made, tortilla that looks and tastes like what you'd cook at home. And, they're often hot out of the kitchen. They go that fast.

After supplying four companies that drive from Phoenix every day to pick up their order, Mi Casa's conveyors keep grinding away to keep up with the steady stream of locals that grab packages almost as quickly as they are cooked. This can amount to almost a ton of flour on a busy day, 900 pounds on a slow day. On the

Friday or Monday near a holiday weekend, Mi Casa can't keep up.

"Our tortillas have gone all over the world," Bertoldo said, naming such faraway places as Alaska, England, Africa and Russia.

Mi Casa's line-up of products includes white corn and flour tortillas, with lard or with vegetable shortening. Their specialty, whole-wheat flour tortillas, has a faithful following. Bertoldo reported, "People say they are the best they've tasted."

"Tortillas can make or break a meal," advised Bertoldo. "When it comes to Mexican food, if you want the taste, you need lard. Save your calorie-counting for something else."

Photos opposite page: From top, (1) Owner, Manuel Bertoldo, (2) Mi Casa's retail store Above: Bertoldo and his son, Michael outside the factory Below: Panorama and inserts of tortilla production workers.

El Charro Restaurant
(928-428-4134) 601 W. Main Street, Safford

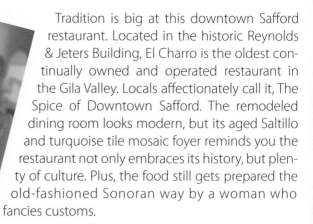

Tradition is big at this downtown Safford restaurant. Located in the historic Reynolds & Jeters Building, El Charro is the oldest continually owned and operated restaurant in the Gila Valley. Locals affectionately call it, The Spice of Downtown Safford. The remodeled dining room looks modern, but its aged Saltillo and turquoise tile mosaic foyer reminds you the restaurant not only embraces its history, but plenty of culture. Plus, the food still gets prepared the old-fashioned Sonoran way by a woman who fancies customs.

For one thing, Chef Mary Lou Alva has cooked for the restaurant since the early 1970s. Alva, who describes herself as "a fast cooker," comes to work every morning at 7 and prepares all the food by noon. She uses her favorite well-worn pots and pans and she cooks the food on a stove that she had moved to the restaurant from her kitchen at home.

"I still measure after all these years," Alva shared. "It makes a difference."

Alva creates some popular dishes. One menu specialty, Chalaca, starts with shaping *masa* (handmade corn dough) into a bowl shape, deep frying the dough, and then filling it with beans and red or green chile topped with cheese, onions and lettuce. Refried beans (about 20 pounds a day), cooked a long time with a little salt – "That's what makes them so good," Alva interjected – then refried with a little oil, remind patrons of their childhood. Her enchilada sauce is made from scratch and has a following.

"I cook, blend and cook some more," Alva hinted about the sauce's secret.

Would she share the recipe? Alva laughed but only divulged, "Well, I have shared the recipe with a few favorite customers."

Photos opposite page: From top, (1) Owners Michal and Dalton Overstreet (2) Johnny Jurado and servers
Above: Combination plate with cheese enchilada, burro and deep fried taco

Casa Mañana
(928-428-3170) 502 S. US 191, Safford

In 1951, there were two places to eat in town: Casa Mañana and the Star Café (currently El Coronado). On a Friday and Saturday night, people lined up to wait for their coveted table at Casa Mañana. The restaurant became a favorite thanks to the gracious owners, "Gabby" and Emma Gabaldon.

Gabby did all the socializing, sitting at a door-side table with the jukebox blaring in a ubiquitous cloud of cigarette smoke while Emma managed the kitchen. The shredded beef was a customer favorite. Over the years, and different owners, recipes changed and the Gabaldon favorites disappeared. But when present owner, Diane Hoopes, purchased the venue, she tracked down as many of the Gabaldon's original recipes as she could.

"It was always a handful of this and a pinch of that and how it looked" said Hoopes. "We had a cook trained by the Gabaldons recreate the dishes. She scooped and we measured. Then we had Gabaldon customers taste test the food for two weeks before we opened to make sure we had the goods."

Julie Cluff, the restaurant's receptionist, concurred her favorite, the Shredded Beef, comes as close as she remembered it during the Gabaldon days. With mission accomplished, Hoopes resurrected other recipes.

"We have several old-Mexico style recipes you can't get anywhere else," Hoopes said. The old-style *rellenos* served with a signature red onion sauce is probably the oldest recipe in the area. The Sonoran Enchilada, another old-Mexico recipe, is a *masa* patty covered with the restaurant's signature enchilada sauce and sprinkled with scallions and chopped green olives. The older customers love these recipes."

Originally a home built in the 1940s, the ivy-covered restaurant still has the brickwork foyer and the cozy stone fireplace from when the Gabaldons owned it. And the restaurant becomes a real party place,

just like old times, when a number of birthdays are celebrated in the house. The community fondly remembers the original Casa Maña-na and Hoopes, a fourth generation Gila Valley resident, is making sure they don't have to forget.

*Photos opposite page: From top, (1) Statute of Mario Mareno Cantinflas from the original Casa Mañana (2) Chef Adam Hoopes (3) Casa Mañana serves classic Mexican fare, plus some different dishes, such as this Sonoran enchilada, old Mexico style. **Above:** Chimichanga, a house specialty, one of ten different kinds offered*

Taco Taste
(928-428-3414) 1827 W. Thatcher Boulevard, Safford

The Little Place With the Big Taste has "been here forever", manager Connie Peck said. As in decades. What started out as a Del Taco, evolved into a Taco Time and now, Taco Taste. And it lives up to its name.

Though it's technically fast food, everything is made from scratch – from the popular Nacho Grande to tacos by the dozen to the homemade salsa. The latter sometimes gets ordered by the cupful.

"We had a guy who used to buy our salsa by the cup and drink it right down," Peck exclaimed. "Everyone loves the hot sauce."

Manager Connie Peck helps kitchen staff

Everyone also loves the food. Period. Stick around awhile in the eatery and you'll get the idea. The service-station-signal that there's yet another car at the drive-up window rings constantly. People drop into the small eating area all day. This is the kind of fast food that can wreak havoc with a diet. Especially if the order includes a chimi, flauta, or cinnamon chips. Or the Super Taco Burro.

"We have a lot of older people come back and ask if we still have the Super Taco Burro," Peck smiled. "They talk about how they had it when they were back in high school."

Yes. Taco Taste still serves the Super Taco Burro. The oldie-but-goodie has crushed up corn chips, beef taco meat, cheese and lettuce wrapped in a tortilla. Now you really get the idea of what Taco Taste is all about. Yes, it's pure comfort food. And, yes, it's dangerously convenient. But it is good.

Nacho Grande & Cinnamon Chips

Salsa Fiesta

(520-384-4233) 1201 W. Rex Allen Drive, Willcox

Gladys Olsen and her daughter, Jennifer Regensberg, opened Salsa Fiesta because, Olsen said, they always stopped at the Mexican food restaurant in Douglas when they'd go to the fair and "wondered why we couldn't have one in our town." Once they opened Salsa Fiesta, they couldn't find a dependable cook. The ladies quickly learned if they were going to make it, they had better learn to cook Mexican fare themselves. Once they started, Jennifer showed an innate talent.

"Jennifer likes to be creative," Olsen said. "Rice and beans are good and popular, but Jennifer shines when she can get creative. There's a big argument where her talent for cooking started – with her grandmother, her home economics teacher, or the 4-H Club. It's certainly not me."

While Jennifer's tastes lean toward fine dining, trying out tastes and trends the two ladies learn about when they travel to food shows across the nation, Olsen likes the more soulful style from the barrio. Over the years Olsen has made several trips to South Tucson to get ideas, ask questions and bring food home to pick apart and figure out ingredients. Also, they buy local when they can.

"We like to support our local people," Olsen explained. "The soil and water in the area make a distinctive difference."

The restaurant serves Bonita Beans grown just down the road, tomatoes from nearby Eurofresh Farms, wine from Coronado Vineyards a few miles east, fresh handmade tortillas from Mexico and habanero peppers from a local grower. Jennifer added she prefers the naturally smoky flavor of the habanero, but not necessarily the heat.

Jennifer then tossed out habanero facts as if she were reading a food encyclopedia reciting how many units on the heat-measuring Scoville scale the habanero contains (around 400,000) compared

Photos opposite page: From top, (1) Gladys Olsen and her daughter Jennifer
Regensberg (2) Delicious salad creations are very popular on the menu
Above: Shrimp salad on mixed greens with Tequila Corralejo, neat.

to the jalapeño (up to 8,000), how many to use for each gallon of salsa (a dozen) and how many for a super-hot salsa (one pepper for each tomato).

And then Jennifer added, "Too much heat could stop a person's heart if they

are not used to it. Some regulars ask me to make a super-hot salsa for them, but I won't."

Jennifer, however, does make seven different salsas (totaling four gallons) each day for Salsa Fiesta's salsa bar. The most famous, and popular, salsa is her *pico de gallo*, but Olsen added, "She makes a mango salsa that's just delightful."

Photo above: Taco, tortilla and rice plate.

Hilda's Kitchen and Meat Market
(928-359-1771) 115 Railroad Boulevard, Duncan

When you step inside Hilda's kitchen, the scene might bring you back a few decades to that neighborhood store where you used to pick up a gallon of milk, a basic veggie or a pound of hamburger at the meat coun-

ter. You can do all that at Hilda's, plus you can get a house-made Big Daddy (an exclusive dish served at venues along Arizona's Salsa Trail) or green chile burros.

"People really like the Mexican food," owner Hilda Goeking said. "They want me to put in more tables."

Presently, Hilda's has only two tables – one by the kitchen and one in the front of the store. Most people order to go. But more often than not the restaurant turns into a meeting place when the customers file in.

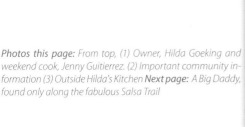

Hilda's Kitchen
We're going to
have Menudo Every
Saturday at 8:am.
Thank you!

Phone: 359-1771.

Under

"People come and go all day long," said Goeking, "but they're starting to hang around, sit down and talk and talk and talk."

This scenario happens again and again. And when it does, Dina Duarte, Goeking's daughter who runs the kitchen, cooks a meal for them.

It's a perfect match, this mother and daughter team that looks very much like a case of "girls just like to have fun." Except these girls know how to turn out a tasty meal. And when they're not cooking they stock the shelves. After all, this is a grocery store and meat market, too.

*Photos this page: From top, (1) Owner, Hilda Goeking and weekend cook, Jenny Guitierrez. (2) Important community information (3) Outside Hilda's Kitchen **Next page:** A Big Daddy, found only along the fabulous Salsa Trail*

P.J.'s
(928-865-3328) 307 S. US 191, Clifton

Jackie Norton and her late husband, Pete, started P.J.'s "on a whim." Jackie cooked for the first four years and developed her own recipes. Thirty years later, P.J.'s remains a favorite with strong, loyal customer base.

"The community has been so good to me," Norton said. "On my first day, we were open from 5 a.m. to 5 p.m., and I grossed $71.62. It paid my expenses and the waitress. Since then, it's been a consistently good business."

So good and so consistent, one of her first customers continues to eat there every day, and several more have become daily diners. Even her staff sticks with her. Norton's first waitress, Nona Powell, just retired after 30 years. Current staff has racked up as much as 15 and 20 years.

P.J.'s red chile enchilada made with its secret sauce, which has been perfected over the years, is the restaurant favorite along with the Green Chile Chicken. However, Norton said P.J.'s "hamburgers are such a calling card. People ask, 'What do you do to make them so good?' and I answer, 'Nothing. That's the way they should be made.'"

P.J.'s goes through two to three gallons of salsa and five gallons of red enchilada sauce daily. Most of the time the salsa makes a perfect accompaniment for the 50 dozen corn tortillas P.J.'s fries up fresh each day for chips. Sometimes, however, the salsa ends up in some unplanned places.

Along the Salsa Trail - Real Arizona

"One day," Norton started, "as one of our waitresses carried two gallon jars of our red salsa across the room, one slipped from her grip and hit the floor. The lid came off when the jar hit the floor and the salsa volcanoed out all over the place covering one of our regulars, 80-year-old Rosie.

"Rosie was drenched," said Norton. "The waitress felt awful, but I couldn't stop laughing. He looked so funny with salsa dripping from him. It was all over his face and his clothes. He just sat there, in silence. This just mortified the waitress.

"We took off his glasses to wipe his face – it was hot stuff, and we wanted to get it off him quickly – and he had two circles around his eyes that were not red," Norton recalled. "Well, the sight of him just made me laugh more. We didn't know if he was mad or not. He just sat there, not saying a word, as we cleaned him off."

Norton finished the Señor Salsa-moment story with a happy ending. Rosie came back later for dinner, wearing the same clothes he had on at lunch.

"I knew he wasn't mad when I saw the salsa-stained clothes," Norton said with a smile. "I told the waitress, 'You have nothing to worry about.'"

Norton summed up the reason P.J.'s is such a success: "Good food and good service. It's a clean and pretty little restaurant."

Except for those occasional Señor Salsa moments.

Photos page 37: *From top, (1) Owner, Jackie Norton, (2) P.J.'s, for more than 30 years, a neighborhood fixture in colorful Clifton.* **Page 38:** *from top: (1) Nona Powell came to work the day P.J.'s opened (2) P.J.'s interior during lunch time.* **This page:** *Green Chile Chicken - a house specialty.*

GIMEE'S

(928-687-1517) • AZ 75, York (Located just north of milepost 395)

Ed Scott laughed when he thought about the key chains he ordered that claimed, We're number one because there's no one else. The only restaurant in the don't-blink-your-eyes-or-you'll-miss-it community of York, located in the scenic Black Hills, not only lives up to the key chain's claim by demographic default, but its food lives up to the "number one" boast.

"People often say, 'We feel like we're coming to your home' when they eat here," Ed's wife, Holly, said. "They leave notes saying, 'Good food!'"

The Scotts opened the restaurant 20 years ago after kicking the idea around for a while. Ed had a friend in Duncan who had a restaurant and Ed thought one just might work in York.

"Either we were going to do it," Ed described how they decided to open Gimee's, "or kick ourselves every time we went by when someone else did."

The Scotts built the restaurant themselves, which led to its unusual name. *Gimee* memorializes all the times Ed would say to Holly, "Gimee the hammer," or "Gimee a nail," and so on. They also built a menu with original recipes they perfected through the years – from the crepe-like chile rellenos (which aficionados should not miss) to the customer-favorite chicken fried steak and salad bar, to the build-your-own hamburger with fixins' from the hamburger bar. Everything served from Gimee's kitchen is house made, and with local ingredients when available.

Those hamburgers come in half-pound sizes, and many customers order a double. Some go beyond a pound.

"These two guys were in some kind of food-eating contest," Ed recalled a particular incident, "and ordered a triple half-pounder."

"With fries and dessert, too," Holly added. "When they got the ticket, one of them said, 'I could feed my whole family for this price.'"

Along the Salsa Trail - Real Arizona

Along the Salsa Trail - Real Arizona

Gimee's takes only cash or checks. One customer, caught without either, actually left his wife as collateral while he went back to Safford to gather the payment. Everyone joked, What if he doesn't come back? The man did come back with payment in hand, to collect his wife. An ATM machine on the premises should alleviate any similar scenarios.

*Photos opposite page: From top, (1) Owners Ed and Holly Scott. (2) One of Ed's many paintings (3) Gimmee's gets crowded at dinner time; **Above:** A happy Gimmee's server with two "Big Daddys".*

41

SAN SIMON CHILE CO.
(928-428-1490) 5256 S. US 191, Safford

"You know the peppers are done when the skin turns black, bubbles, cracks and starts to fall off to show the meat," said San Simon Chile Co. owner, Jane Wyatt, as she watched a batch of *Big Jims* do their dance over the fire.

The roasting happens by way of a mesh metal drum that turns methodically over an open flame. The fuel that stokes the flame sounds like an airplane taking off and the chile peppers start to mimic the sound of popping corn. As the chiles heat up, they snap and pop when their skin bursts. A delightful pepper pungency wafts when the chiles near perfection, after 10 to 15 minutes of flame time. These *Anaheim* chiles, the mildest of the three varieties Wyatt sells, are destined for burritos, enchiladas or to be eaten right out of the bag (a practice common among chile aficionados).

Wyatt's jalapeño peppers (called *Early Jalapeño*) are the hottest in the state. You won't find them in the supermarkets – or anywhere else, for that matter. Wyatt described the Arizona's Salsa Trail's exclusive as having "too much teeth" for most people's heat tolerance and doesn't produce well to sell profitably. But it does produce a following.

Spending a little time at Wyatt's outdoor market gives a quick lesson in chile pepper basics. You not only learn facts like how climate and soil make a difference in the taste of the chile, you might pick up a little lore from the customers, such as how the curl at the tip of a chile indicates a hotter pepper. You might even get an object lesson or two.

"When you break open the pod," chile lover, Charlie Torres from Morenci demonstrated by cracking a *Big Jim* open, "the yellow vein holds the heat. Just a touch of the tongue to it brings heat that lasts for a l-o-n-g time."

Torres demonstrated again with a daredevil touch of his tongue on the demon heater vein. But Torres likes what the pepper does, explaining after popping a fresh one in his mouth, "you get a feeling similar to a runner's high."

Indeed, chiles do have a pleasurable effect because their heat-causing ingredient, capsaicin, creates an endorphin rush in the body. Endorphins produce an opium-like euphoria, a feeling of intense well-being. Like opium, the capsaicin causes you to crave more. Unlike opium, this addiction is good for you. Research shows chiles can increase oxygen, help prevent blood clotting, heal ulcers, kill toxic food-borne bacteria, prevent cancer cell proliferation in cultures and relieve pain.

"I've got to have my chiles," one customer affirmed the addictive nature. "I haven't been able to cook the same since we ran out," his wife added.

"This is a familiar story," Wyatt said. "Two or three sacks for a household are normal."

"You can tell you're developing a habit when you start getting into three and four sacks of chile taking up all the freezer space," the man continued as if a participant in a self-help group. "We had to buy another freezer."

All this explains why Wyatt's outdoor chile market buzzes with activity in August when the green fruit on the chest-high chile plants becomes perfect for the picking. She and her brother, Joe Blair, produce about 20 acres of chile peppers. In a good year, they'll get 7,000 to 10,000 pounds of peppers per acre. Green chiles come first and then they allow some to ripen on the vine into red chiles for roasting or sun drying. Gas dried chiles, the method used most often, don't have as good a taste as sun dried and gives some people heartburn.

Wyatt will tell you it's backbreaking work to harvest the fruit pods. Harvesters start picking with the sunrise and stop with the heat. They also have to endure blisters acquired when a pod breaks open in their hands. And if the weather turns foul, as Arizona weather tends to do during the monsoons, and pelts the fields with hail, the chile crop will suffer. It's enough to give everyone the jitters.

All this hard work pays off when the chile pepper community swarms around the burlap bags of just-picked peppers then watches and breathes in the fragrance as their chosen chiles roast over the open fire. The patrons nibble on jalapeño salsa and crackers or pop a chile or two, neat, and boast about their chile prowess. Oh, sure, some complain about the labor of love peeling the chiles requires or recite a litany of chile blues when their stash of frozen chiles run out; but all in all, Wyatt's is the place to be every August. After all, Señor Salsa will be there, and it's a lot of fun.

*Photos page 42 : From top, (1) Owner, Jane Wyatt talks chile peppers, (2) loading peppers into roaster, (3) removing roasted chiles, (3) color of freshly roasted chile peppers; **Page 43:** Chile harvest happens during the heat of summer; **Page 44:** From top, (1) Jane with brother and partner, Joe Blair, (2) Jane's farm in the shadow of Cochise's Head, (3) Jane holds a handful of her special Early Jalapeño peppers, (4) Jane on her original Super M Farmall Tractor; **Page 45:** Bags of freshly picked green chiles at the San Simon Chile Company; (inset) Jane with a jar of Señor Salsa*

Now

for

the

Recipes...

SALSA TRAIL FOOD TIPS

Roasting and Toasting

Roasting a pepper, tomato, tomatillo or spice brings out a rich, complex flavor. Roasting concentrates sugars in the tomato and peppers. With green chiles, it's *de rigueur*.

"A lot of people who don't know chiles may use an unroasted green chile," advised Jane Wyatt, owner of San Simon Chile Co. "but that's not appetizing. The chile needs to be roasted and peeled to produce the fullest flavor."

Fresh chile peppers

You can roast fresh chiles several ways: on an outdoor grill, over a stove top flame, under a broiler, or in a heavy skillet over medium heat. First clean the chiles. Turn the chiles to make sure the skin is blistered and blackened all over without burning the flesh.

When done, place the chiles into a plastic bag and seal until cool. The skins should peel off easily. Toss the seeds if you want less heat, and don't touch your eyes or face until you have washed your hands thoroughly.

Toasting dried chile peppers

Clean the chiles. Place them atop a rack on a baking sheet in an oven at 250 degrees. Remove when the chiles start to release their aroma and darken (about 5 minutes). Don't let the chiles burn or they will turn bitter.

To rehydrate chiles, place them in a bowl and cover with boiling water. Let them soak and soften about 20 minutes.

Tomatoes and Tomatillos

Wash, dry and stem the tomatoes; husk the tomatillos. Proceed as with chile peppers.

Spices

Place spices in a small pan over medium heat and toast until fragrant and browned, but not burned. Use toasted spices right away; do not store.

Fresh versus Processed

Several recipes call for powdered spices (such as garlic powder) or canned vegetables (such as tomatoes, corn and green chiles). Many readers prefer fresh ingredients. For the best-tasting results, below are substitutions you may make to successfully replicate any recipe with fresh ingredients.

SPICES

You may prefer to use fresh herbs and spices. If you cannot, or prefer not to, use fresh spices or dry your own; keep in mind spices purchased at a grocery store are generally not as fresh as spices bought in bulk from a spice or an herb shop.

Along the Salsa Trail - Real Arizona

We have found El Guapo brand spices (available at many grocery stores and Mexican markets) are flavorful alternatives to fresh or freshly dried herbs and spices. Also, Mi Casa Tortilla Factory has spices and cornhusks (for tamales). San Simon Chile Co. has dried red chiles and dried chipotle chiles and powder.

1 tsp dried herbs = 3 tsp fresh herbs
1 clove garlic = 1 tsp fresh minced garlic = 1/4 tsp garlic powder

TOMATOES

Canned tomatoes have been peeled and heat-treated. You can replicate them by boiling fresh tomatoes for a minute, or until the skins crack; remove them from the boiling water, cool and peel. Roma tomatoes work best for cooking Mexican food.

Whether using canned or fresh tomatoes in a recipe, it's best to seed and core the fruit, unless you need the extra liquid to add moisture to a recipe or flavor a broth.

1 fresh tomato = about ¼ cup seeded, cored and chopped
1 pound of fresh tomatoes = about 5 Roma tomatoes
A 16-oz can tomatoes = 2 cups undrained tomatoes = 1 cup drained tomatoes

GREEN CHILES

One 4-oz can equals 1 large or 2 small roasted, peeled, seeded and chopped green chile(s).

Arizona's Salsa Trail Recipes

Dining along Arizona's Salsa Trail gives you a pretty good idea of what it would be like to join a *familia* gathering. The food is down-home good and the atmosphere casual and fun.

Though Tex-Mex in style, the food has enough Mex to over-shadow the Tex with heavy traditional influences. And it's made the old fashioned way from long hours in hot kitchens by chefs that like to cook. You may not find a mango-on-a-stick (a peeled mango on a wooden stick doused with lime juice and sprinkled with chile pepper powder) or corn-on-the-cob with mayonnaise, lime juice and chile pepper powder or churos, but you will find handmade tortillas, extraordinary salsas and sauces, tortas, sopaipillas and a traditional Mexican dish here and there.

The following original recipes have been gathered from several sources. Many are from the restaurants and venues that comprise Arizona's Salsa Trail. Several have come from venues along the Salsa Trail and area residents. Señor Salsa even added a few of his own. The compendium of recipes and tips will give you all the information you need to create a meal you might order along Arizona's Salsa Trail, and more.

Fideo Sopa

– One of Johnny Jurado's special Friday meals for the staff; "Basically", Johnny described the one-skillet dish, "it's shell pasta, ground beef, chopped tomatoes, onions and spices."

Along the Salsa Trail - Real Arizona

BURRITOS
FILL FLOUR TORTILLAS WITH PINTO BEANS, CHEESE, RED CHILE SAUCE. FOLD TORTILLA. TOP WITH MORE SAUCE AND CHEESE. BAKE 30 MINS – 350°

BLUE CORN ENCHILADAS
FRY BLUE CORN TORTILLAS IN HOT OIL 5 TO SECS. DRAIN. LAYER WITH CHOPPED RED ONION, SHREDDED JAR CHEESE, ENCHILADA SAUCE ON OVENPROOF PLATE. BAKE 300° 10-15 MINS. GARNISH WITH LETTUCE.

STEAK QUESADILLAS
PLACE ON FLOUR TORTILLA SLICED STEAK, CHOPPED SCALLIONS, CHEESE. FOLD TORTILLA OVER. COOK BOTH SIDES IN BUTTER. SERVE WITH SOUR CREAM & SALSA.

CARNITAS
IN 2 TBS OIL. SAUTE TILL SLIGHTLY DRY SHREDDED ROAST PORK, ½ C. WATER, GARLIC POWDER, OREGANO, CUMIN, RED CHILE POWDER, SALT & PEPPER. ROLL IN CORN or FLOUR TORTILLA. GARNISHES: SALSA, GUACAMOLE, LETTUCE, TOMATO, SOUR CREAM.

GREEN CHILE SAUCE
1. TBS. SHORTENING
½ C. CHOPPED ONION
2 TBS. FLOUR
1 C. CHOPPED GREEN CHILE
1 C. CHICKEN BROTH
1 TSP GARLIC POWDER
¾ TSP SALT
SAUTE ONION IN SHORTENING. ADD FLOUR, COOK 1 MINUTE. ADD REMAINING INGREDIENTS. SIMMER 20 MINS –

El Charro Johnny's Hot Jalapeño Salsa
(Makes 1 cup cooked; 2 cups raw)

Johnny Jurado, El Charro's main dish-out person for the last 25 years, is always experimenting with different salsas. He shared his favorite, this recipe for green salsa, which the restaurant serves. Johnny said the ingredients could be used raw or boiled. Raw, he explained, gives the salsa a greener taste; cooked, his preference, mellows the salsa.

Jurado, who grew up with four older brothers, joked, "I had to stay in the kitchen in order to get something to eat and ended up learning how to cook." Jurado brings a special meal he cooks at home to the restaurant every Friday (see *Fideo Sopa*, left). This gives the staff something different, and special, to eat.

5	Jalapeño peppers (seeded and chopped for raw salsa)
2	Tomatoes (chopped for raw salsa)
1 medium	Onion, peeled (chopped for raw salsa)
2 cloves	Garlic, peeled and minced
1 tsp	Mexican oregano
½ tsp	Cumin, ground
	Salt to taste

For cooked version –

- Boil the Jalapeño peppers, tomatoes and onion for 10 to 15 minutes or until *al dente*.
- Drain and discard the water.
- Let cool.
- Chop and follow directions for raw version.

For raw version –

- Combine chopped jalapeño peppers, tomatoes and onion.
- Add seasoning and mix thoroughly.

Lorraine's Pico de Gallo

Lorraine's Pico de Gallo
(Makes about 2 cups)

The entire repertoire of recipes owner, Ray Villalobos, makes at La Casita restaurant is a secret. Ray's wife, Lorraine, offered this recipe. She
said this tastes great on corn chips or you can use it on grilled steak.

4	Roma tomatoes, seeded and diced
2	Jalapeño peppers, diced
½ cup	White onion, diced
½ cup	Cilantro, chopped
2	Limes
	Garlic salt to taste

- Mix tomatoes, jalapeño peppers, onion and cilantro in a deep bowl.
- Squeeze the juice from both limes into the mixture.
- Add garlic salt as needed.

Matiana's Salsa
(Makes 1 quart)

Lupe Holler, who works at Eurofresh Farms in Snowflake, AZ, won the company's *Mexican Food Recipe Contest* with this family recipe. Holler named the salsa for her mother, who owned a Mexican food restaurant.

"My mother played with different ways to make a salsa that her customers would enjoy," Holler said. "At the time, she did not know how much of a success it would be until customers started asking to buy it in jars to take out. My friends and acquaintances have asked why I haven't put it out in the local market."

1 clove	Garlic, peeled and chopped
7	Jalapeño peppers
8	Eurofresh Farms tomatoes
¼ bunch	Cilantro (remove stems; they can cause bitter taste)
	Salt to taste

- Wash the jalapeño peppers (remove the stems), tomatoes and cilantro.
- Roast the tomatoes and peppers in a skillet, turning occasionally until they become almost completely black. Do not peel; skin adds character to the salsa. Set aside.
- In a blender, add garlic clove and one-half of the roasted tomatoes and all the peppers; blend until smooth.
- Add the rest of the tomatoes and cilantro and press the pulse button three times to mix and keep thick consistency.

The Empies' Favorite Salsa
(Makes about 5 cups)

The late artist, Hal Empie, lived in several towns along Arizona's Salsa Trail – Safford, where he was born and grew up; Solomon, where he and his late wife, Louise, managed the Best Drug Store; and Duncan, where he managed, then owned, the Best Drug Store. He and Louise closed the Duncan drugstore and moved to Tubac in 1986 where they opened the Hal Empie Studio and Gallery. His daughter, Ann Empie Groves, now runs the studio.

Ann submitted this favorite family recipe. Hal Empie's granddaughter, Kathy O'Donnell, is the chief salsa maker in the family.

3 cans	Del Monte Mexican Tomatoes (12.5 oz.), drained
5	Jalapeño peppers, seeded and chopped fine
3 cloves	Garlic peeled and minced
½ medium	Yellow onion, peeled and chopped
1 4-oz can	Chopped green chiles
½ tsp	Chile powder, hot or mild
½ tsp	Ground *cuminos* (cumin)
½ tsp	Garlic salt (optional)
1 to 2 dashes	Cayenne pepper

Mix all ingredients and refrigerate until ready to serve.

COOK'S TIP: *If the specific tomatoes the recipe calls for aren't available, we recommend diced tomatoes, as shown in the photograph. The chunks of tomatoes complement the diced ingredients perfectly.*

Salsa Roja Asada
(Makes 2 cups)

Almost all the fresh ingredients used in this thick salsa are roasted. This adds some resonance to the flavors. The salsa has a little kick if you use one or two jalapeño peppers. You can dole out the salsa on just about any one of your favorite Mexican dishes for extra flavor or eat it solo on chips.

8	Fresh Roma tomatoes
1	Green chile pepper
1	Yellow onion, sliced thick, roasted close to the flame or broiler until charred on both sides, and chopped.
2 cloves	Garlic, peeled and minced (about 2 tsp)
2 Tbsp	Lime juice
1 tsp	Lime zest
½ cup	Fresh cilantro leaves, washed (no stems)
½ tsp	Cumin seeds, toasted and ground
¼ tsp	Kosher salt (or more to taste)
¼ tsp	Fresh cracked black pepper

- Roast the tomatoes, discarding roasting liquid. Let cool. Slip off the peels, separate the fruit from the core. Discard the core and juice.
- Roast the chile, peel, discard stem and seeds.
- Place tomatoes, chile, onion and minced garlic into a food processor and pulse until just mixed.
- Add the lime juice, lime zest and cilantro leaves; pulse a couple times.
- Add the cumin, salt and pepper and pulse a few times to mix.
- Serve immediately, or refrigerate up to 24 hours.

Secret Salsa Verde
(Makes about 3 cups)

Diane Hoopes, owner of Casa Mañana Restaurant, uses fresh ingredients in her menu's recipes that are precisely measured. This salsa, she said, is "great on eggs, as a marinade or as a dip."

1 lb	Tomatillos, husked and rinsed
1 clove	Garlic, peeled and finely chopped
¼ medium	White onion, chopped
¼	Jalapeño pepper, with seeds
1 tsp	Kosher salt
4 sprigs	Cilantro, washed and chopped
	Fresh cracked black pepper to taste

- Place the tomatillos in a medium saucepan and add enough water to cover.

- Bring to a boil and cook until tender, about seven minutes. Drain.

- Combine all ingredients except for cilantro in a food processor or blender, and puree until smooth.

- Add the cilantro and pulse a few times to mix.

Pesto in a Molcajete*

* The molcajete is the Mesoamerican mortar and pestle, traditionally carved out of a single block of porous basalt volcanic rock. Like cast iron cookware, it retains flavors and brings complexity to the seasoning of anything made in it.

Simpson Hotel Pesto Salsa
(Makes about 3 cups)

Owner/innkeeper Deborah Mendelsohn serves this pesto salsa with breakfast at the Simpson Hotel. The recipe, which she's perfected over the years, blends Mediterranean and Latin American tastes and traditions.

Marinade (prepare in advance):

2-5 cloves	Garlic
1 or 2	Jalapeño peppers
¼ cup	Sun-dried tomatoes
½ cup	Extra virgin olive oil
1 Tbsp	Balsamic vinegar
½ tsp	Oregano (fresh or dried)

Fresh ingredients to add just before serving:

1 bunch	Fresh basil, stemmed and chopped (about 1 cup)
½ bunch	Fresh cilantro, stemmed and chopped (about ½ cup)
1	White onion, chopped
½ cup	Tomatoes, chopped
Salt	
Pepper, fresh cracked	

- Roast the garlic and jalapeño peppers in a heavy skillet over medium heat; turn frequently until all sides are browned; remove from heat, cover with a dish-cloth and let sit for 30 minutes or more. When cool, peel the garlic and chiles. Taking care not to get the chile oils near eyes or nose. Remove the chile seeds if desired (to avoid excessive "heat").

- Mince the garlic and chile together.

- Put the minced ingredients in a *molcajete** or small ceramic bowl.

- Add the sun-dried tomatoes, olive oil, balsamic vinegar and oregano.

- Add salt and fresh-cracked pepper to taste.

- Cover and allow the ingredients to marry their flavors at room temperature for at least two hours, preferably overnight.

- After marinating, remove the sun-dried tomatoes, roughly chop them and then add back to the marinade.

- Add the fresh ingredients (above) just before serving and mix well.

Serve with chips, eggs, pan-roasted potatoes, on pasta or over steamed vegetables.

Guacamole
(Makes about 2 cups)

If the Salsa Trail was in Brazil, you might find avocados in your ice cream. In the Philippines, you might add one in milk with a little sugar. Aztecs called the fruit *ahuacatl*. The Spaniards, who preferred their avocado with a little sugar and salt, corrupted the Aztec name into *aguacate*. Along Arizona's Salsa Trail, guacamole is essentially Mexican using the basic ingredients of *aguacate*, cilantro, chile pepper, tomato, cilantro and salt. The recipe below adds a few spices for variety.

2 ripe	Avocados, peeled, seeded and mashed
1	Roma tomato (about ¼ cup), seeded and chopped
1	Jalapeño pepper, roasted, seeded and finely chopped
1 large clove	Garlic, peeled and minced (about 1 tsp)
¼ cup	Cilantro leaves, washed and chopped
½ tsp	Cumin seed, toasted and ground
½ tsp	Mexican oregano, crumbled
	Kosher salt and fresh-cracked pepper to taste
1	Lime, juiced

- Combine all ingredients except the lime juice and mix well. Adjust seasoning to taste.
- Squeeze the juice of 1 lime into the guacamole and mix well.
- Serve immediately or refrigerate up to 24 hours.

COOK'S TIP: *The avocado will discolor and turn brown when exposed to air. If refrigerating, place plastic wrap right on the guacamole to keep color fresh.*

Tortilla Chips
(Make as needed)

We owe the delight of biting into a crispy tortilla chip topped with salsa to the late Los Angeleno tortilla factory owner, Rebecca Webb Carranza. She and her husband, Mario, automated the darling of the Mexican dinner table with a tortilla-making machine at their El Zarape Tortilla Factory in southwest Los Angeles.

The machine, which made tortillas 12 times faster than the most proficient hand, produced a number of misshaped tortilla rejects that Carranza at first threw away. Instead of tossing them out one day, Carranza cut the misshapen disks into triangles and fried them up as a snack for a party. A star was born, and she ended up selling bags of the salted chips, which she called "Tort Chips," for a dime. When tortilla chips appeared on the table at Mexican food restaurants, Señor Salsa couldn't believe his good fortune.

Corn oil (or canola oil for flour tortillas)
Corn (or flour) tortillas cut into eighths and laid flat on a cotton towel
Salt

- Pour a quarter- to half-inch of oil into a thick-walled saucepot or an electric skillet and heat to 350 to 370 degrees.
- Drop in a small batch of wedges and fry until crispy 1 to 2 minutes.*
- Remove with a slotted spoon and drain on paper towels. Repeat until done.
- Salt chips lightly while still warm.

 * Fry only a few chips at a time so the temperature of the oil remains even

COOK'S TIPS: *You can refrigerate the corn oil for reuse if you –*

- *Don't use copper or iron pots.*
- *Keep the cooking temperature below 375 degrees.*
- *Strain out all food particles before storing the oil.*
- *Store the used oil in the refrigerator in a sealed container.*
- *Throw the used oil out when it turns dark and gets gooey.*

The oil should stay fresh enough for reuse for two to three weeks.

Lazy B Ranch Tamale Pie

*W*hen Alan Day located this recipe, he and his sister, retired U.S. Supreme Court Justice Sandra Day O'Connor, tried it and reported, "It's the same one we had when we were kids. It brought back fond memories." Alan and Justice O'Connor grew up on the Lazy B Ranch some six miles from Duncan.

"My mother (Ada Mae) used to cook this recipe all the time," Alan said. "It's good when you have unexpected company because it only takes about a half-hour to whip up."

Above: Sandra Day O'Connor and her book "Lazy B" about life on her Arizona ranch, written with her brother Alan Day (Random House, New York, N.Y. 2002).

Ada Mae's Lazy B Ranch Tamale Pie
(Serves 6)

2 lbs	Ground beef
3 Tbsp	Chile powder
1 tsp	Garlic powder
1½ cups	Onion, peeled and chopped
½ cup	Black olives, sliced and drained (2 oz can)
2½ cups	Diced tomatoes (28 oz can), drained
1½ cups	Corn (15 oz can)
2 Tbsp	Butter
4 cups	Water
1 cup	Yellow cornmeal
	Salt and pepper to taste
3 cups	Grated cheddar cheese

Preheat oven to 350 degrees

- In a large skillet, brown ground beef and chopped onion.
- When meat is no longer pink, add chile powder and garlic.
- Add drained olives, tomatoes and corn; mix well and simmer 10 minutes.
- In a saucepan bring water to boil, reduce to simmer and add cornmeal in small amounts while stirring with a whisk to avoid lumps.
- Continue stirring until mush thickens.
- Stir in butter and set aside.
- Butter a 9 x 13-inch pan or ovenproof casserole dish.
- Spread cornmeal mush for bottom layer.
- Spread meat mixture for next layer.
- Sprinkle cheese for top layer.
- Bake uncovered for 45 minutes.
- Let rest 15 minutes before serving.
- Serve with salad or coleslaw.

COOK'S TIP: *If you use fresh rather than canned ingredients add at least 1 tsp salt to the meat sauce. To liven the cornmeal mush, add ½ pound of sautéd chorizo and mix it in the mush before spreading the layer.*

Casa's Famous Fish Tacos
(Makes 6 tacos)

Casa Mañana is the only one of the Salsa Trail's restaurants to serve fish tacos – the ultimate street food in Baja.

1 quart	Canola oil
2 cups	Prepared tempura batter (or your favorite recipe)
8 oz	Alaskan pollock or cod fish cut into half-inch strips
1 cup	Flour
2 cups	Fresh shredded cabbage
1	Lime, cut into wedges
½ cup	Chipotle mayonnaise (see recipe below)
6	Flour or corn tortillas, grilled
½ cup	Pico de Gallo, freshly made

- Heat canola oil in an eight-quart Dutch oven or deep fryer to 350 degrees.
- Mix tempura batter and let stand 10 minutes.
- Put flour on a plate and dredge each piece of fish in the flour, coating completely with flour; shake off excess flour.
- Dip each floured piece of fish into the tempura batter, and coat completely.
- Carefully place the battered fish into the hot oil and fry until crispy, about 3 to 5 minutes. Do not fry too many pieces of fish at a time in order to keep the temperature of the oil consistent.
- Remove fish and put on a paper towel to drain.

Assemble tacos by laying out warm tortillas in a large pan. Place a piece of fish on each tortilla. Drizzle 1 tsp of chipotle mayonnaise over each piece and pile cabbage on top. Garnish with a scoop of Pico de Gallo and a lime wedge.

Chipotle Mayonnaise

1 cup	Mayonnaise
½	Chipotle chile in adobo sauce
½	Ancho chile in adobo sauce
¼ cup	Cilantro leaves (fresh)
	Salt and pepper to taste

Put all ingredients into a food processor and blend until creamy.

a Different Steak Pico . . .

O ne of Chalo's signature dishes is Fajitas – steak, chicken and shrimp. This recipe combines the steak fajita ingredients into one glorious creation. Marie Freestone, one of Señor Salsa's official recipe testers reported, "It's not only beautiful to look at but also a pure delight to eat. My 86-year-old mother shared it with me and stated, 'I'll never want to eat a plain steak again.' It was beef in the garden for sure."

Chalo's Steak Pico
(Serves 2)

Pico de Gallo –

16 oz	Certified Angus beef top sirloin steak pan-seared on each side and cooked to order on char-broiler grill
½ cup	Green bell pepper, diced
½ cup	Tomato, diced
½ cup	Red onion, diced
1 bunch	Cilantro, chopped
2 to 3	Jalapeño peppers, diced (if spicy heat is desired)
1 or 2 cloves	Garlic, peeled and finely chopped
	Salt to taste
½ cup	Cheddar cheese, grated
½ cup	Monterey Jack cheese, grated

- Preheat oven at 450 degrees.
- Mix bell pepper, tomato and onion together.
- Add garlic salt to taste and chopped cilantro.
- Spread evenly over cooked pan-seared steak.
- Mix cheddar and Monterey Jack cheeses together.
- Place the cheeses on top of the *pico de gallo*.
- Melt cheese in oven (5 to 10 minutes).
- Serve with refried beans, Spanish rice, warm corn or flour tortillas.

Chalupa
(Serves 8 to 12)

Karen Wiley entered this recipe in *Arizona's Salsa Trail Recipe Contest*. She said it makes the perfect recipe for her large family gatherings. "You can make everything early," Karen said, "feed a large crowd and enjoy the gathering yourself without being stuck in the kitchen."

3 lb	Boneless round roast
1 lb	Raw pinto beans, cleaned and washed
2 cloves	Garlic, peeled and chopped (about 2 tsp)
2 Tbsp	Chile powder
1 Tbsp	Cumin seed, ground
1 tsp	Oregano
2 (4-oz) cans	Chopped green chiles (or 1 cup roasted, peeled and chopped fresh green chiles)
½ to 1 tsp	Salt
	Cracked pepper to taste

Condiments –

Corn chips	Grated cheddar and/or Jack cheese
Red onions, chopped	Lettuce
Tomatoes, chopped	Avocado, sliced
Ripe olives, sliced	Hot sauce

- Place pinto beans into a slow cooker; cover with water.
- Stir in garlic, chile powder, cumin, oregano, salt and pepper.
- Place roast on top and add more water to cover.
- Cook on low until the meat is tender, about 6 hours.
- Remove roast, shred the meat with a fork and return the shredded meat to the slow cooker.
- Cook with the lid off until thick, about 1 hour.
- Serve the meat mixture in small bowls over a bed of corn chips along with any and all condiments.

Bill Civish, the mastermind of Arizona's Salsa Trail, created this recipe. His hobby is cooking good food. Civish's talents go back to the small town in Utah where he grew up. When his mother died, he had to cook dinner for his dad. The women in the neighborhood took it upon themselves to teach this teenager how to cook. Each day, one would meet him at the bus stop (so as to preclude his escaping their lessons) and have him help her make dinner, which he'd take home. These ladies, most from "the Old Country," were not your average Americanized cooks. Consequently, he learned how to prepare Italian, Greek and Mexican meals. Civish said he never fully appreciated the special understanding he learned about foods from these ladies until much later. Now, no one turns down an invitation to his dinner table. Especially when he's cooking some of his favorite Mexican foods.

Chile Verde Burrito
(Serves 6)

5 lb	Pork shoulder roast
3 Tbsp	Cooking oil
1 medium	Yellow onion, peeled and chopped
2 cloves	Garlic, peeled and minced
1 can	Tomatoes (28 oz)
1 can	Green chile sauce with pork (15 oz)
2 Tbsp	Mexican oregano
1 tsp	Crushed red pepper flakes
½ tsp	Onion powder
½ tsp	Garlic powder
1 tsp	Ground cumin
4 cups	Chicken stock, fresh or low sodium
8 large	New Mexico chiles, roasted, peeled, seeded & chopped
1 dozen	Large flour tortillas, heated
2 cups	Mexican blend cheese (cheddar and Jack), shredded
1	Lemon, juiced
1 cup	Cilantro, chopped or green onions, sliced, for garnish
	Salt and pepper to taste

Note: Pork shoulder roast can be prepared in a Crock-Pot® or slow cooker on low setting for 8 hours.

- Rub pork shoulder with salt and pepper.
- Heat cooking oil in a 5-quart Dutch oven and brown roast on all sides. Re move from the pan.
- Add onions and garlic and cook until onions are opaque.
- Return roast to pot and add chicken stock, whole tomatoes (hand crush) with liquid, garlic powder, onion powder, cumin, oregano leaves and crushed red peppers. Cover and simmer 3 hours.
- Remove roast from pot, reserve liquid, let meat cool and then shred with two forks.
- Add shredded pork, chopped chiles and 2 cups reserved liquid to a 10-inch fry pan. Bring to a simmer and cook 20 minutes.
- Add lemon juice to pork mixture.
- In a small saucepan, heat canned green chile sauce.
- For each burrito, spoon a generous 1/3-cup pork mixture in the center of each tortilla. Top with 2 Tbsp cheese. Fold tortilla over each end of filing and roll. Place on oven proof plate.
- Spoon green chile sauce over burritos and cover with cheese.
- Put burrito plate into a 450 degree oven until cheese is bubbling and melted.
- Garnish with cilantro or green onions.

COOK'S TIP: *You will have leftover meat. Civish creates another meal out of it by adding potatoes and carrots to make a stew he sops up with fresh tortillas.*

Green Chiles and Eggs
(Serves 4)

From the recipe file of June Potter Palmer, courtesy of Joanne Arnold

If you stay at the Potter Ranch Bed & Breakfast, owner/inn-keeper June Palmer might serve this for breakfast.

12 oz	Canned green chiles, diced
1 lb	Monterey Jack cheese, grated
4	Eggs
4 Tbsp	Flour
¾ cup	Evaporated milk
	Salt and pepper to taste

Preheat oven to 350 degrees

- In an 8 by 8 inch square pan, layer chiles and cheese.

- Combine eggs, flour, salt, pepper and milk and beat well.
- Pour over cheese and chiles.
- Bake at 350 degrees for 30 minutes, or until set.

Green Chile Chicken Enchiladas
(Serves 4 to 6)

One of the most popular dishes at P.J's Restaurant in Clifton is the Green Chile Chicken Enchiladas. Owner, Jackie Norton, said she has a hard time making her recipes in small quantities because she's so used to preparing them for the restaurant in large amounts. In honor of this menu item, Señor Salsa revealed his favorite version below.

Sauce –

4 Tbsp	Butter
½ cup	Flour
1 cup	White onion, peeled and chopped
3 cups	Chicken broth, homemade or low-sodium canned
¾ cup	Green chile peppers, roasted, peeled and chopped – or – (Norton's preference) 3 or 4 jalapeño peppers
2 cloves	Garlic, minced (about 2 tsp)
2 tsp	Mexican oregano, crumbled
	Salt and fresh cracked pepper to taste

- Melt butter in a heavy saucepan.
- Add flour, mix thoroughly and cook over medium heat for 2 minutes.
- Add onions (and jalapeños) and sauté until soft, about 5 minutes.
- Whisk in chicken broth, bring to a simmer and stir until smooth.
- Add roasted green chile peppers, garlic, Mexican oregano, salt and pepper (both optional); simmer 20 minutes. Cool. You may puree in a food processor if you prefer no chunks.

COOK'S TIPS: *For a lighter sauce, cut the amount of butter and flour in half. You may refrigerate sauce two days before using it or freeze it.*

Enchiladas –

8	Corn or flour tortillas (regular size)
¼ cup	Corn oil, heated (optional)
½ cup	Sour cream
4 cups	Chicken, fully cooked and shredded
3 cups	Cheddar cheese, grated

- Preheat oven to 350 degrees.
- Pour ½ of the sauce into a 9-inch by 12-inch baking dish, spread evenly.

To assemble enchiladas (double portions for large flour tortillas) –

- Brush a tortilla with some of the hot corn oil or 1 tsp of sauce, place ½ cup of chicken, 1 Tbsp of sour cream (optional) and some grated cheese on it, roll it up and lay it the baking dish; repeat.
- Top with remaining sauce and grated cheese.
- Cook at 350 degrees for 30 minutes.
- Let stand for 5 to 10 minutes before serving.

La Paloma Chile Rellenos
(Serves 6)

6   Eggs (separate yolks and whites)

12   Green chile peppers roasted, skinned, slit lengthwise on one
        side and seeded

1 cup   Flour

12 oz   Cheddar cheese cut in 1-inch-thick strips
        Enough safflower oil to fill a deep fryer halfway

Preparation:

- Stuff each chile pepper with 2 strips of cheddar cheese; set aside.
- Start heating oil to frying temperature.
- Whip egg whites until they meringue.
- Beat eggs yolks and fold into the meringue.
- Drop a stuffed green chile in deep bowl filled with flour and bury
  completely in the flour.
- Dip the flour-coated chile in the meringue batter and completely
  coat it.
- Carefully place the battered chile pepper into the deep fryer of hot
  oil.
- Fry each chile until golden brown.
- Drain on paper towels.

COOK'S TIP: *Award-winning chef, Janos Wilder of Tucson, Arizona, suggests in his book, The Great Chiles Rellenos Book (Ten Speed Press 2008), that you fry rellenos in a thick-bottomed pan or cast-iron skillet with ¼-inch of canola or corn oil at 360 to 370 degrees F. Keeping the oil at this temperature cooks the rellenos correctly – too cool an oil temperature causes the rellenos batter to absorb the oil; too hot and the batter cooks too quickly and the filling doesn't heat properly. The canola or corn oils are healthy and relatively inexpensive.*

Carne Asada

Mi Casa Mexican Bar-B-Q
(Serves 4 to 6)

Manuel Bertoldo's classic recipe below begs for his large flour tortillas to hold all the goodies you can put inside.

Marinade –

2 cloves	Garlic, peeled and minced
1 Tbsp	Olive oil
3 or 4	Lemons
	Salt and pepper to taste

- Juice the lemons.
- Add garlic and salt and pepper to taste.

Tortillas –

2 lbs	7-bone roast, cut (against the grain) into 6-inch strips or London broil or Sirloin steak
8	Green chile peppers, roasted, seeded and peeled
8	Corn tortillas
½ cup	Butter (optional)

Condiments –

1 cup	Sour cream
1 or 2	Avocados, cut into strips
½	Medium onion, peeled and sliced
1 to 2 cups	Cheddar and/or Monterey Jack cheese, grated
8	Green onions
2	Tomatoes, chopped
1 bunch	Cilantro, chopped

- Marinate strips of beef for an hour.
- Grill to desired doneness.
- Heat each tortilla on the grill and then butter (optional).
- Fill with a roasted and peeled green chile and a strip of meat.
- Add condiments of choice.

"Many years ago, the most popular eating spot in the Gila Valley was a small, dilapidated building in Solomonville, simply called 'Shorty's.' When we went to eat there, especially on the weekends, we had a long wait in line. So everyone always took a deck of cards with them to make

the time pass. No one seemed to mind because the Mexican food at Shorty's was so good it was worth the wait. His specialties were Red Chile and Green Chile. I have these recipes now because of my cousin, Irene Owens of Safford. When Shorty died, the restaurant closed. Irene went to Solomonville and got Mary, Shorty's wife, and brought her to her home to show her how to make the Chiles. I consider myself lucky to have them." Reprinted with permission from "A Pioneer's Daughter Remembers – DeConcini Family Cookbook (1882 – 1988)"

The following two recipes taken from the DeConcini cookbook are included for the adventurous cook. This is classic cooking "by how it looks" and "if it feels right." Shorty's method of cooking leaned toward simple, uncluttered tastes.

Shorty's Chile Verde
(Serves 6 to 10)

In this recipe Ora suggests, "This recipe is good in burritos but may also be used with refried beans."

1	Pork loin roast (4 to 5 lbs), cut into 1-inch squares with a little fat left on
1 can	Ortega Chiles (4 oz, more if you want it hotter)
1	Yellow onion, chopped
2	Ripe tomatoes, chopped (optional)

- Brown meat in a large heavy skillet.
- Simmer meat with onions (uncovered) and tomatoes (optional) until all moisture is gone.
- Cover with hot water. If you want a more savory dish, use chicken stock (preferably fresh and low sodium), instead of water
- Add chile and simmer until pork is tender.

Serve with grated Monterey Jack and/or cheddar cheese, warm tortillas and limes.

COOK'S TIPS: *If you are using tomatoes, we suggest Roma, cored but not seeded. We recommend adding enough water to cover the meat two inches and simmer the meat loosely covered for about two hours.*

Much of the water will reduce; the final outcome should have the consistency of a thick stew. You may shred the pork cubes with two forks after cooking a couple hours, and you may add spices (such as Mexican oregano, cumin, coriander or cinnamon), more water if necessary and continue cooking another half hour.

Shorty's Red Chile
(Serves 10)

Along with the recipe for Chile Verde (previous page), Ora DeConcini included this coveted recipe from Shorty's Cafe. The directions are in first-person.

2 cellophane bags	Dried red chiles, one hot and one mild. *
5 lbs	Lean pork cut into cubes, with most fat removed.
3 Tbsp	Garlic salt
	A little flour

We always fixed the paste for the Red Chile the day before because it is a job in itself. We would clean the chiles, and then bring them to a boil until they were soft. Next we would blend them and strain. Half of this mixture would be enough for one batch and we froze the rest.

*We cooked the pork in a heavy pan in a small amount of fat until all the moisture was completely gone, about an hour. When the meat got dry, we added salt and garlic salt to taste, and then completely covered the pork with flour, coating it well. Then the red chile mixture was added with enough water to cover the meat two to three inches. Cook approximately two hours until pork is tender. ***

* These exact chile ingredients are unknown, but they may well be El Guapo brand California Red Chiles (16 oz) or New Mexico Red Chiles (16 oz) and Chile de Arbol (2 oz).

COOK'S TIPS: *To make a single batch of the "chile paste," use 8 to 10 dried chiles and 2 or 3 arbol chiles. We recommend roasting them for a few minutes (until the chiles darken slightly, but before they turn black). Rehydrate the chiles by pouring a cup of boiling water over them and soaking until soft (about 20 minutes). Remove the chiles from the soaking water, place them in a food processor and puree, adding enough soaking water, to make a thick paste.*

As always, if you want a more savory dish, use chicken stock (preferably fresh and low sodium), instead of water. We recommend replacing the garlic salt with 3 garlic cloves, minced and salt to taste (start with ½ to 1 tsp of kosher salt). You can add other spices, such as Mexican oregano, cumin, coriander or cinnamon. If you do, add them during the last half-hour of cooking.

** Reprinted with permission from *"A Pioneer's Daughter Remembers – DeConcini Family Cookbook (1882 – 1988)"*

One of the most popular dishes on Arizona's Salsa Trail, and a reoccurring specialty at the restaurants, is Cheese Enchiladas. The secret, well guarded at each restaurant, is in the sauce. Señor Salsa recommends the following enchilada sauce.

Cheese Enchiladas
(Serves 4)

10	Dried red chile peppers
3 Tbsp	Olive oil
1 medium	Yellow onion, chopped
2 cloves	Garlic, peeled and chopped (about 2 tsp)
2 tsp	Mexican oregano, crushed
1 tsp	Cumin seed, toasted and ground
½ tsp	Coriander seeds, ground
4 cups	Chicken stock, fresh or low sodium canned
	Fresh cracked sea salt and black pepper to taste
1 tsp	Sugar (preferably raw, unrefined)

- Wipe the red chiles clean with a dry cloth and then roast them until they give off an aroma.
- Remove chiles from the oven, let cool slightly. Crack the stems off and shake the seeds out. Discard seeds and stem. For hotter chile sauce, retain some or all of the seeds.
- Place the chiles in a bowl, pour boiling water over them and let steep for 20 minutes. Strain and set aside.
- Heat the olive oil in a heavy saucepan.
- Sauté the onion over medium heat for 2 minutes.
- Add the garlic, oregano, coriander and cumin and sauté 3 minutes.
- Add the chile peppers and chicken stock; simmer for 20 minutes.
- Turn off heat and let the sauce rest for about 15 minutes.
- Add salt and pepper to taste
- Place sauce in a food processor in 2 to 3 batches and puree until smooth; strain if necessary.
- Add 1 tsp sugar and pulse a few times to mix.
- Use immediately, refrigerate up to two days or freeze.

Enchiladas (Preheat oven to 350 degrees)

5 cups	Enchilada sauce
1 lb	Grated good-quality cheddar cheese
8	Flour tortillas (or 4 large)
½ cup	Cilantro leaves

- Pour enough sauce (about 1 cup) to cover the bottom of a 9-inch x 13-inch baking dish.
- Spread 2 Tbsp of sauce on a tortilla (¼ cup for large).
- Place 3/4 cup of grated cheese and a few cilantro leaves on the tortilla and roll up, keeping ends open (1 cup for large), Place in the baking dish. Repeat.
- Pour remaining sauce over tortillas and sprinkle with remaining cheese.
- Bake uncovered for 25 minutes; remove from the oven and let rest 15 minutes before serving.

Bisque

Red Pepper Bisque
(Serves 4)

This recipe won the Soup/Salad division of the *Arizona's Salsa Trail Recipe Contest*. People around Safford say winner Jo Ann Tallerico should have her own cookbook. After you taste this bisque, you'll understand why.

2 large	Red bell peppers (or 3 small)
1¼ cup	Onion, diced
8 Tbsp	Butter
1 large	Garlic clove (or 2 small), minced
1 tsp	Ground chipotle pepper (or ½ tsp fresh ground red chile pepper)
3 cups	Chicken stock
1 cup	*Crema Mexicana* or heavy whipping cream
1 Tbsp	All-purpose flour
	Salt to taste

Thin tortilla strips or cornbread croutons, cilantro or green onions for garnish.

- Roast and blister the skin of the whole red bell peppers, peel, seed and cube (approximately 1¼ cups).
- In a saucepan, sauté on medium heat the diced onions in 4 Tbsp of butter until tender, then add the garlic and sauté 1 or 2 minutes more, stirring constantly so the garlic doesn't burn.
- Place the cubed red bell pepper, sautéed onions, ground chipotle and garlic in a blender and fill with cold or room temperature chicken stock, leaving 2 to 3 inches of room at the top. Blend until smooth (3 or 4 minutes). You may strain the liquid through a sieve or cheesecloth to remove any unblended vegetables.
- Put the red pepper broth back into the clean saucepan and add any remaining chicken stock. Bring to a simmer (do not boil) for 5 minutes. Add salt if desired.
- In a small microwave-safe dish, melt 4 Tbsp butter. Whisk 1 Tbsp of flour into the butter, and then slowly whisk the mixture into the soup until it has a creamy texture.
- Simmer the soup for 5 minutes to remove any flour taste.
- Remove soup from heat, and add ½ cup crema or whipping cream to the soup.
- Add more salt if necessary.
- Ladle the soup into a shallow bowl and place cornbread croutons or tortilla strips in the center of the surface of the soup.
- Garnish with *crema* or whipping cream (use a squeeze bottle to make patterns) and cilantro or chopped green onions.

Albondigas Soup

Gladys Olsen, one of the owners of Salsa Fiesta, said this family soup recipe is great anytime. "If you are ill," she added "it seems to perk you up better than chicken soup – so the story goes."

Salsa Fiesta's Albondigas Soup
(Serves 6)

Stock –

1 Tbsp	Olive oil or butter
1 medium	Yellow onion, diced
1 quart	Water
2 bundles	Green onions, diced (use green and white parts)
1 can	Green chiles (4-oz), diced
1 can	Tomatoes (28-oz), chopped
1 tsp	Garlic powder
1 tsp	Cumin, ground
1 Tbsp	Mexican oregano
2 Tbsp	Raw white rice
	Salt and pepper to taste
½ bunch	Cilantro
1 or 2	Limes, cut into wedges

- In a medium stockpot, heat the oil or butter and sauté diced onion until limp.
- Add the rest of the ingredients. Bring to a steady boil.
- Add meatballs (recipe below), dropping into boiling soup one meatball at a time, while keeping the stock at a boil.
- When all meatballs are added, reduce heat and add rice. Taste to adjust seasonings.
- Let simmer 45 minutes.
- Serve steaming hot. Top with cilantro and wedges of lime on the side.

Meatballs –

2 pounds	Lean ground beef
2	Eggs, beaten
2 Tbsp	Raw white rice
½ cup	Flour (more or less)
1 pinch	Garlic powder
	Salt and pepper to taste

- Combine all ingredients.
- Form into small meatballs, 1½- to 2-inches each.

COOK'S TIPS: *Use beef or chicken stock – preferably fresh or low sodium – for a more savory soup. You may add 3 tsp finely chopped fresh mint (1 tsp dried) to the meatball mix.*

Chipotle !

San Simon Chipotle Marinade
(Makes enough for 1 ½ to 2 pounds steak or chicken)

Jane Wyatt started growing green chiles for pharmaceutical and cosmetic purposes. The green chiles she grows in the San Simon Valley are known for their excellent quality and flavor. This recipe uses smoked jalapeño (chipotle) peppers.

1	Lime
3	Oranges
3 cloves	Garlic, peeled and finely chopped (about 3 tsp)
2 to 3	Chipotle chiles, remove stems and seeds and chop (see Cook's Tip)
½ tsp	Cumin seeds, ground or freshly milled
½ tsp	Black pepper, ground or freshly milled
2 tsp	Mexican oregano
½ tsp	Salt
2 Tbsp	Wine vinegar

- Juice the lime and oranges.
- Combine all ingredients in a food processor or blender.
- Puree until smooth.

COOK'S TIP: "On the chipotles," Wyatt advised, "I don't soak them when I make the marinade, I just put them in my Cuisinart® and grind thin, almost like a powder. But it would not hurt to soak them, and especially in the citrus juices. You can also use the chipotles that are canned in the grocery store, which will already be soft."

Chile Corn
(Serves 4)

If you like sweet corn, the lime in this recipe takes the word sweet to new heights. The red chile adds color and a trace of heat. For more kick, you can sauté a half to whole finely-chopped fresh jalapeño pepper.

2 cups	Fresh corn-on-the cob (2 to 3 ears)
1 tsp	Fresh, coarsely ground dried red chile pepper
1 clove	Fresh garlic, minced (about 1 tsp)
1 Tbsp	Unsalted butter
3 Tbsp	Fresh lime juice (2 small limes)
1 tsp	Lime zest
¼ cup	Fresh chopped cilantro
	Salt and pepper to taste

- Shuck the corn, remove the silk and cut the kernels off the cob.
- Heat the lime juice, unsalted butter and minced garlic in a pan over medium heat until the butter melts. Add the corn, coarsely ground red chile pepper (or finely chopped fresh jalapeño pepper) and salt and pepper; sauté for 3 minutes.
- Remove from heat and mix in the lime zest and cilantro. Serve immediately.

Flour Tortillas
(Makes 6 large tortillas)

"There are lots of right ways to make tortillas," said Alva Peeler, born in Chihuahua, Mexico in 1939. "My mother makes this recipe with milk instead of water." Peeler, who now lives in Duncan, lived in Mexico until she graduated from high school. She shares this favorite recipe plus some invaluable information about the process of making tortillas. "Many people who made this recipe have told me, 'This is the first time I could make flour tortillas.'"

3 cups	Flour
¼ tsp	Baking powder*
1 tsp	Salt
3 Tbsp	Canola oil
1 cup	Lukewarm water

* Some people use 1 Tbsp baking powder for the same amount of flour.

- Mix all ingredients (you may use a food processor).
- Knead the dough 2-3 minutes. For tender tortillas, mix as little as possible. We like to "toughen" tortillas so they will hold up well for burros, so I knead mine until the dough is elastic.

- Form dough into six balls and let stand for a few minutes.
- Roll and cook on a grill that is set between medium and hot. If you cook them too slowly, they will be too dry and crispy; if it's too hot, they will burn. I cook mine on the first side just until it forms small bubbles on the top, turn and cook completely on the second side, turn back to the first, and finish cooking. Other people cook it completely on one side, then the other. I sometimes press down briefly on the tortilla with a paper towel or clean cloth while it cooks on the final side. This helps it to rise. The steam helps cook it. Be careful not to burn yourself on the steam.
- Put each tortilla aside to cool until warm, then it can be stacked.
- Store cooled tortillas in a Ziploc® bag.

COOK'S TIP: *You can freeze tortillas by sealing a stack of them in an airtight container or plastic bag. When you're ready to use them, remove what you want, wrap in a clean towel and microwave for 30 seconds to 1 minute; or, place them in foil and heat in a conventional oven preheated to 250 degrees for 5 to 10 minutes*

Pinto Beans
(Makes 5 to 6 cups of cooked beans)

Bean recipes come in many shapes and sizes. Señor Salsa prefers no competition from side dishes and recommends pintos be prepared at their simplest.

3 qts	Water (or enough to cover beans 2 to 3 inches)
1 lb	Pinto beans (2 cups)
2 Tbsp	Lard, saltless butter or vegetable oil
1 to 2 tsp	Salt (optional)

- Pick over beans for small pebbles and dirt, wash several times, add enough water to cover and then soak overnight.
- Drain the soaking liquid, put beans into a large pot with lard, saltless butter or oil, add enough water to cover 2 to 3 inches.
- Bring to a boil, lower heat and simmer until just tender (about 2 ½ hours).
- Add salt (optional) and simmer a half-hour longer.
- Strain the beans and reserve their liquid.

COOK'S TIPS:

- *Older beans take longer to cook.*
- *The higher the altitude at which you're cooking the beans, the longer the cooking time you'll need.*
- *Hard water requires longer cooking times.*
- *Adding salt at the beginning of cooking toughens the beans.*
- *To reduce the beans' infamous gastric distress, discard soaking liquid before cooking. Research has shown little of the nutrients are lost with this water, but the hard-to-digest carbohydrates are.*

Jícama Salad

Jicama Salad
(Makes 4½ cups)

Actually a member of the legume family, jicama has the taste and texture of a water chestnut. The vegetable makes a refreshing base for a salad and excellent complement for hot, spicy foods.

3 cups	Jicama, peeled (use a paring knife, not a potato peeler) and julienned
1 large	Ripe mango, peeled, seeded and chopped into cubes (about 1¼ cup)
2	Scallions (green stalk only), finely chopped
¼ cup	Fresh, chopped cilantro leaves
3 Tbsp	Fresh lime juice
1 tsp	Lime zest
1 clove	Garlic, crushed (about 1 tsp)

- Combine the jicama, mango chunks, green part of scallions and cilantro.

- Combine the lime juice, lime zest and minced garlic, and then add to the jicama mix.

- Toss well. Refrigerate at least an hour (up to 24 hours) before serving.

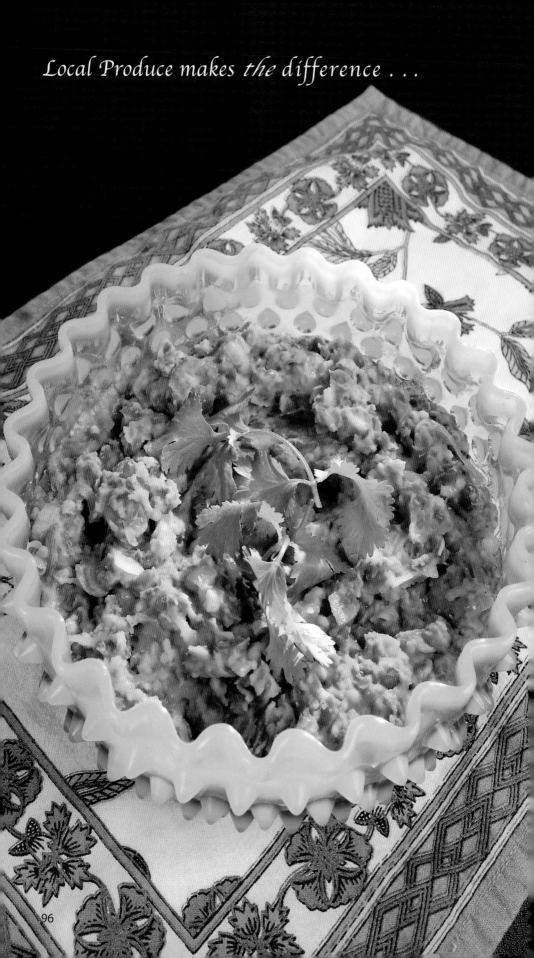

Refried Beans
(Serves 8 to 10)

3 Tbsp	Lard or vegetable oil
½ cup	Yellow onion, diced (optional)
1 clove	Garlic, minced (optional)
1 lb	Pinto beans, cooked (reserve the cooking liquid)
1 cup	Cheddar and/or Monterey Jack cheese
	Salt and pepper
	Cilantro

- Heat lard or oil over medium heat in a heavy skillet. Add onions and sauté for four minutes or until they start to get tender.
- Add minced garlic and sauté for 1 minute.
- Add a quarter of the pinto beans and mash into the oil mixture. Add more beans, along with some of the cooking liquid and continue mashing. Repeat until the beans are incorporated and the mash is smooth.
- Lower the heat, add the cheese and blend; garnish with cilantro.

Lisa's Mexican Fiesta Cake

MEXICAN FIESTA CAKE

In early 2008, *Arizona's Salsa Trail Recipe Contest* was launched, inviting the community to share their favorite family recipes. The judges, who included award-winning Chef Terry Dagnino from San Carlos Casino's Apache Grill, chose eight different recipes. Next, students from the culinary class at Pima High School tested the recipes and the two teachers, Carol Jones and David Cluff, judged the results. Recipes that could be successfully duplicated and tasted as good as they looked have been included in the book. This one, submitted by Lisa Clifford, won the grand prize.

Cake:

1	Yellow cake mix
1	Instant lemon pudding (4 oz package)
1 can	Fruit cocktail (16 oz), including syrup
1 cup	Shredded and sweetened coconut
4	Eggs
¼ cup	Oil

- Preheat oven to 325 degrees.
- Grease a 9 x 13-inch cake pan.
- Blend all ingredients and beat 4 minutes at medium speed.
- Pour into greased 9 x 13-inch pan and sprinkle with Topping (below).
- When cake is done, let it cool for 15 minutes and top with Butter Glaze (below).

Topping:

½ cup	Brown sugar, packed
½ cup	Pecans, chopped

- Mix together and sprinkle on top of cake just before baking.

Butter Glaze:

4 oz	Butter
½ cup	Sugar
½ cup	Evaporated milk
1 ½ cup	Shredded and sweetened coconut

- Combine butter, sugar and milk; boil for 2 minutes.
- Stir in coconut.
- Spoon mixture over warm cake slowly, allowing it to seep into the cake.

Angie's Buñuelos

Buñuelos
(Makes about 10)

Though *buñuelos* simply means doughnuts, the recipe has turned into a special Christmas tradition for Angie Montoya. Angie is known around Duncan as one of the best cooks in town. She ran Angie's Cocina in Art's Meat Market, now Hilda's Kitchen & Meat Market, on Arizona's Salsa Trail in Duncan. This recipe handed down by Angie's mother, and also included in the P.R.I.D.E. Society Historical Community Cookbook, has been in the family for generations.

Syrup:

2 cups	Dark brown sugar
1	Cinnamon stick
1 cup	Water

- Boil all the ingredients for 30 minutes. Set aside.

Buñuelos:

½ cup	Water
1 tsp	Anise seeds
2 cups	Flour
1 tsp	Sugar
½ tsp	Salt
½ tsp	Baking powder
1	Egg, slightly beaten
2 Tbsp	Butter, melted
¼ cup	Milk

- Boil the water with the anise seeds, lower it to a simmer for 2 minutes, and then set aside to cool. Strain seeds and reserve the flavored water.

- Sift dry ingredients together.

- Stir in egg, milk and anise water.

- Add melted butter and mix well.

- Knead dough on a floured surface for about 3 minutes.

- Divide into 1½-inch balls and let stand, covered, with a cloth for 30 minutes.

- Roll out balls of dough on a floured surface to very thin circles four to five inches in diameter.

- Fry in of hot oil (¼ to ½ inch deep at 370 degrees) on both sides until golden brown.

- Drain on paper towels.

- Angie's tradition is to dip the buñuelos into hot syrup. Or, you can place a buñuelo on a plate, ladle hot syrup onto it and top with a scoop of vanilla ice cream or a dollop of fresh whipped cream.

Bush & Shurtz Fried Ice Cream
(Serves 8)

Since fried ice cream is one of the favorite items on the menu, Bush & Shurtz owner, Margie Robinson, often makes several batches of this confection a day. The trick to a perfect outcome is to freeze the cornflake-coated slabs of ice cream until they are rock solid frozen.

. . . a Bush & Shurtz specialty

½ gallon	Vanilla ice cream (block)
2 cups	Milk
3	Eggs, beaten
1 tsp	Cinnamon
2 tsp	Vanilla
1 box	Crushed and sweetened corn flake crumbs

- Cut the block of ice cream into eight equal chunks (first cut lengthwise, then across four times).

- Mix together the milk, eggs, cinnamon and vanilla.

- Dip a chunk of ice cream in the milk mixture.

- Roll the ice cream in the crushed cornflakes to coat completely; repeat milk mixture and corn flakes procedure several times, if necessary, to make sure the ice cream is completely coated.

- Freeze at least an hour or overnight.

- Drop into at least four inches of safflower or other light oil heated to 375 degrees with tongs for half a minute and drain.

- Top with favorite sauce and serve immediately.

Fried Ice Cream

Candied Red Hot Peppers
(Makes 8 candied peppers)

Marina Rauh, who tested several recipes for this book and inspired this one, was fascinated by the bowl of whole candied fruit presented at the end of a dinner when traveling in southern France. "Glacéd fruit has always been a big thing in France and Italy. It looks so attractive. So why not do chile peppers?"

Candied red chile peppers not only make dazzling conversation pieces, they're an unusual dessert for a Mexican dinner. At first bite the candied chile has the chewy consistency of fruit leather, but the chile ends up melting in your mouth, leaving a warm glow behind.

8	Dried red chile peppers
2 cups	Sugar
1 cup	Water

- Cut a little hole in each pepper in an unobtrusive spot a size just bigger than the size of a seed and shake out the pepper's seeds, tapping and rotating the pepper as necessary. For more heat, leave the seeds in. Leave the stems on.

- Clean the peppers with a dry cloth.

- In a wide saucepan, heat the water and sugar over medium-high heat until the sugar dissolves, stirring often.

- Add the peppers, lower the heat and simmer for 20 minutes, or until the peppers turn translucent. You may have to reposition the peppers to make sure each one gets enough time in the sugar water.

- Remove the peppers and drain on a rack for 30 minutes. They will look glassine.

- Transfer the peppers to an oiled sheet of foil to dry further.

COOK'S TIP: *Serving suggestions – Place a candied chile in a dish of rich vanilla ice cream, sorbet or sherbet (lemon, orange or mango would work well). Drizzle with quality chocolate syrup, sprinkle with freshly shaved quality chocolate or top with orange or lemon zest.*

Cowboy Wes' Oatmeal Cookies
(Makes 5 dozen cookies)

Maggie Polen Bryce said this oatmeal cookie recipe has been in her mother's family "forever." Bryce submitted this recipe in *Arizona's Salsa Trail Recipe Contest* and got an honorable mention. One of the secrets to the recipe is soaking the raisins in the liquids to plump them up. Her husband, Wes (a drawing (by Bryce) of him appears on the *Old West Highway Guide*, opposite page), loves to dunk the crispy cookies in coffee.

2	Large eggs, beaten
1 cup	Butter
1 cup	White sugar
1 cup	Brown sugar
1 cup	Pecans, chopped
1 tsp	Vanilla
1 cup	Raisins
2½ cups	Flour
2 tsp	Backing soda
½ tsp	Salt
2 cups	Oatmeal

- Preheat oven to 375 degrees.
- Beat eggs well in a small bowl; add raisins and vanilla. Let soak.
- In a large bowl, mix the other ingredients like biscuit dough with a pastry blender.
- Add egg mixture and mix well. If dough is too dry, add a bit of water until it will stick together.
- Roll dough into walnut-sized balls and flatten them onto a lightly greased cookie sheet with a fork.
- Bake at 375 degrees for 10 minutes.

Chile Pepper Oatmeal Crisps
(Makes about 3 dozen crisps)

On the night of the full moon, Señor Salsa arrived in Maggie Polen Bryce's kitchen and worked a little mischief. He swapped golden raisins for the regular ones Bryce usually uses and then soaked them in chile pepper stock. It was a hit. Then he tinkered with the rest of the recipe to make these Oatmeal Crisps full of chile pepper heat. Full moon or no, chile pepper lovers will not want to miss this hot version of an American favorite.

1 cup	Butter
1 cup	White sugar
1 cup	Brown sugar
2	Large eggs, beaten
2 tsp	Vanilla
1 cup	Golden raisins
4	Dried red chile peppers
1½ cups	Flour
2 tsp	Baking soda
2 tsp	Cinnamon
1 tsp	Fresh ground red chile
½ tsp	Salt
2 cups	Oatmeal

- Preheat oven to 350 degrees
- Put dried chile peppers in a small saucepan, slitting to release the seeds into the pan; cover with boiling water and steep for 20 minutes. Mash a bit with a wooden spoon and let steep for 10 minutes. Strain and reserve the water. Discard the chiles and seeds.
- Add the golden raisins to the chile water and soak until plump.
- In large bowl, cream the butter.
- Add white sugar and brown sugar, beating well after each addition.
- Add eggs, beating after each one.
- Add the vanilla and mix well.
- Sift together flour, cinnamon, chile powder, salt and baking soda; add to the creamed mixture and beat well.
- Stir in the oatmeal.
- Drain raisins and discard the chile water. Stir the raisins into the dough.
- Spoon walnut-sized portions of dough onto a greased cookie sheet, leaving room for the dough to spread.
- Bake at 350 degrees for 10 minutes. Take out of the oven and cool a few minutes before removing crisps onto a rack to cool.

Chile Ganache Cookies
(Makes 3 dozen cookies)

These chocolate cookies, a takeoff on chocolate truffles, make a happy ending for most any Mexican meal. Señor Salsa reports they taste as elegant as the rich confectionery, but aren't as fussy – they travel well and they melt in your mouth, not in your hands.

12 oz.	High-quality bittersweet chocolate
6 Tbsp	Unsalted butter
½ cup	Flour
3 Tbsp	High-quality cocoa
¼ tsp	Salt
1 tsp	Freshly ground red chile powder (or cayenne pepper)
1¼ cup	White sugar
3	Large eggs
1 Tbsp	Orange liquor
1 Tbsp	Orange zest
	Parchment paper for baking

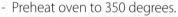

- Preheat oven to 350 degrees.
- In a small saucepan, melt the butter over low heat and add the chocolate. Melt the chocolate, stirring often. Remove from heat and set aside.
- Sift together flour, cocoa, salt and freshly ground red chile powder (or cayenne pepper). Set aside.
- Beat eggs and sugar until pale and thick, about 2 minutes.
- Stir in the orange liquor and the chocolate mixture until thoroughly blended.
- Add the flour mixture and blend well.
- Stir in the orange zest.
- Cover dough with plastic wrap pressed against the mixture and refrigerate at least three hours; preferably over night.
- Form dough into 1½-inch balls and place on cookie sheet lined with parchment paper.
- Bake at 350 degrees for 10 minutes.
- Take cookies out of oven and let rest 5 minutes before placing on rack to cool.

My Mother's Favorite Cake
(Makes a Bundt cake or three 9-inch layers)

When Arizona Ranger and Official Willcox Tour Guide, E. Pierre Brehm, gave permission to use this recipe from the *Rex Allen Museum Cookbook*, he said it not only was his mother's favorite cake recipe, but it usually ends up everyone else's favorite who makes the cake. Pierre reported this cake recipe has been in the family for more than 100 years. He emphasizes the recipe calls for real fruit; berry juice does not count. His fruit of choice is blueberry. We used strawberries in honor of Della Coronado's strawberry cake, served at El Coronado Restaurant.

1½ cups	Sugar
¾ cup	Butter, softened
3	Eggs
3 cups	Flour
3 tsp	Baking powder
½ tsp	Salt
1 ½ tsp	Cinnamon (if using apples)
1 cup	Whole milk
2 tsp	Vanilla
2 cups	Strawberries (one quart), cleaned, hulled and chopped

- Preheat oven to 350 degrees.
- Butter and flour a Bundt baking pan or three 9-inch round cake pans.
- Cream sugar and butter.
- Add eggs, one at a time and beat well after each one.
- Sift together flour, baking powder, salt (and cinnamon for apples).
- Add dry ingredients in two or three portions, alternating with the milk, mixing well after each addition.
- Add the vanilla.
- Stir in the fruit gently until mixed.
- Bake at 350 degrees for 45 minutes or until a toothpick inserted comes out clean.

COOK'S TIPS: *Though this cake is certainly moist enough to eat as it is, we suggest serving it with a little ice cream or fresh whipping cream. If you are baking a layer cake, frost the cake with your favorite butter cream frosting.*

Destinations
Food, Wine and Activities

There's more to the Coronado Trail than the 120-mile road that coils up into the White Mountains from Clifton to Springerville. The entire route the handsome Francisco Vásquez de Coronado traveled in 1540 A.D. began at Compostela, Mexico (just west of Mexico City), meandered around and through Arizona's Salsa Trail, up the White Mountains, eastward to the Rio Grande River and then all the way to Quivira in Kansas. The historic route, then an adventurous quest, still holds plenty of adventure and mystery.

When Coronado started out from his Mexican base on that wintry Sunday morning, he led a flamboyant entourage of 225 caballeros, 60 infantry, a thousand native helpers, some women and children and a handful of servants. Dressed in garments ranging from chain mail and bull hide to brightly colored festival frocks and body paint, the contingent set out with more than a thousand horses and mules carrying provisions or holding the promise of food further down the way.

Once in Arizona, the expedition followed, generally, paths trodden by native peoples that wound their way from the San Pedro River northward over several mountains to the Gila River. During this segment, Coronado said he found the pre-historic ruins of Chichilticalli. The ruins, whose name means red earth, have still not been officially located. But historians think the expedition camped in a gallery of cottonwoods called Eureka Springs near Aravaipa Creek. A ruin near Solomon called Pueblo Viejo may, perhaps, be the mysterious Chichilticalli ruins referred to by Coronado.

The troupe continued northward to the Gila River, passing through some rough and tumble country near the Black Hills Backcountry Byway and the Gila Box National Conservation Area. So harsh became the topography as it climbed northward into the White Mountains, that Coronado reported the journey "troubled the soldiers not a little." The traveling became so wretched, a large number of the animals were lost. "The lambs and wethers lost their hoofs...and (t)en or twelve horses had died of overwork." This is not to mention the human loss, which Coronado reported, "was not a slight loss for the rest of the expedition."

Much of the area around Arizona's Salsa Trail, terra incognito to Coronado when he traveled this way, contains miles of open space. So you never know, just like Coronado, what you'll find along the way. Arizona's Salsa Trail has world-class birding, watchable wildlife, rockhounding sights, historic trails, ancient fir forests, canyons with year-round water and Sonora Desert beauty. Unlike Coronado, who ended his pass through this area starving and bedraggled, you're nowadays only a short drive from civilization...not to mention a good, hot Mexican meal.

Arizona's Salsa Trail Annual SalsaFest, Salsa Glow and Balloon Fest

Each year on the last weekend in September, when the aroma of roasting chiles fills the air and the harvest moon lights the night sky, Graham County celebrates its annual SalsaFest. The festival starts out with a Salsa Glow, when hot air balloons line up on Main Street and light up like lanterns from blasts of propane stoked by each balloon's pilot. The balloons launch early Saturday morning and do their aerial dance, and then festivities follow in Safford's Town Square on Main Street and 8th Avenue.

In between band sets, door prize announcements and dance performances the salsa contest keeps everyone busy. Tables with amateur salsa makers line up in one tent with the promise of cash prizes for the top three salsas. Chefs from the Salsa Trail restaurants vie for the traveling trophy, which gets displayed for a year in the first-place winner's restaurant.

...y and Bill Civish serve their Salsa entry at the SalsaFest.

"Eat this," declared mustachioed Tom Davidson about his salsa to a young man, "and you'll grow a mustache like mine." The young man smiled wanly, rubbed his chin and blushed. A young girl giggled when Davidson said the same thing to her about his handlebar mustache.

Festival-goers graze among the tables of salsa masters with a plateful of tortilla chips in one hand and collecting samples of salsas with the other. Then they find a comfy spot at a picnic bench or under a tree or in front of a performing artist and ruminate on which salsa tastes the best

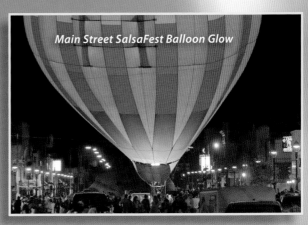

Main Street SalsaFest Balloon Glow

and then share their findings with family and friends. Finally, they mark their winning choices and cast their ballots.

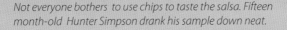

Not everyone bothers to use chips to taste the salsa. Fifteen month-old Hunter Simpson drank his sample down neat.

111

Salsa Trail
Activity Map

1. Aravaipa Canyon

2. Black Hills Back Country Byway

3. Cluff Ranch

4. Gila Box Riparian Conservation Area

5. Haekel Road

6. Hot Well Dunes

7. Klondyke

8. Reay Lane

9. Red Knolls

10. Round Mountain Rockhound Area

11. San Francisco River

12. Swift Trail

13. Willcox Playa

14. Mt. Graham International Observatory

15. Morenci Mine

Please Note:

This map is for orientation purposes *only*. It is *not intended* for land navigation. Detailed USGS 7½ minute topographic maps are recommended for back country and off highway travel.

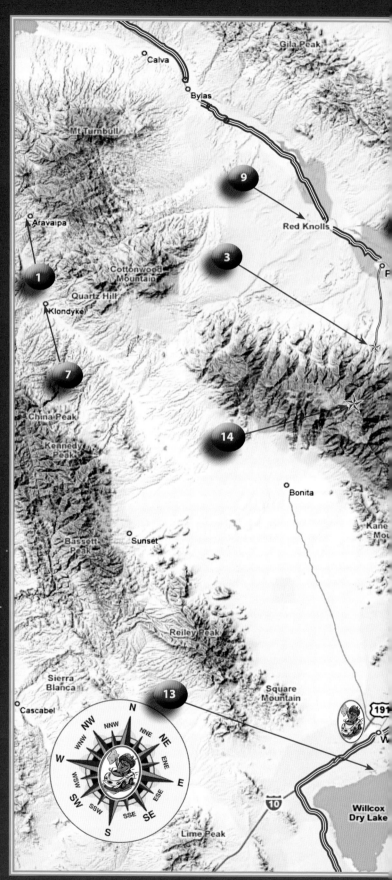

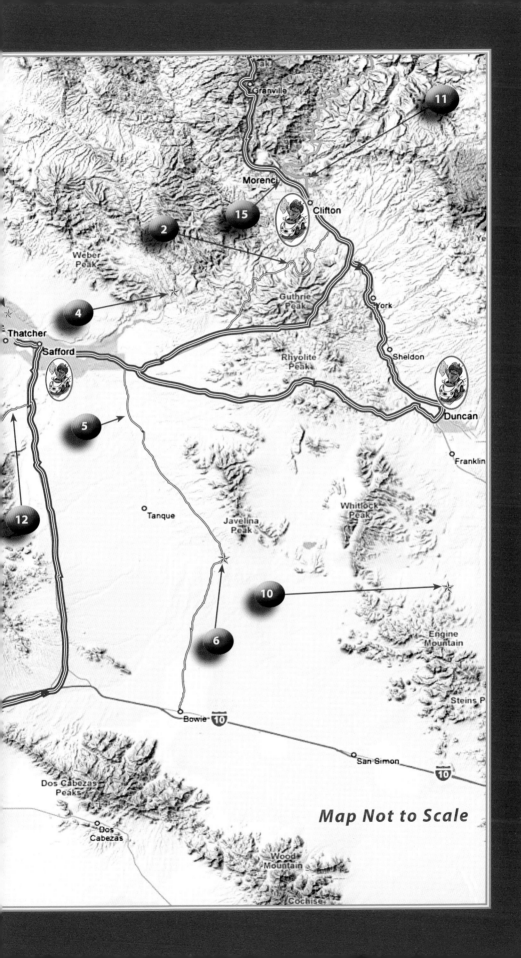

Map Not to Scale

Farms along Arizona's Salsa Trail

Senator Dennis DeConcini vividly recalls his summers in the latter 1940s at his mother's family's farmhouse in Thatcher. "It was there that I spent some of my most memorable childhood days, riding tractors, working and playing at harvesting crops, and gaining exposure to a set of ethics and values that characterized the pioneer farm families of Graham County." From *Senator Dennis DeConcini: From the Center of the Aisle* by Dennis DeConcini and Jack L. August, Jr. © 2006 The Arizona Board of Regents. Reprinted with permission of the University of Arizona Press.

Ethics may remain the same, but farming techniques have greatly evolved. The iconic tractor still chugs along the highways. But you'll also see some new-

fangled deluxe machinery that will have you scratching your head and wondering what task it might accomplish.

The early Euro-American and Mexican pioneers in the Gila Valley discovered about 30 irrigation canals dug by native peoples. A field report written in 1851 by Lt. Amiel Whipple on his survey of the Gila River northeast of Pinal Lalano Mountain (Mount Graham), described what the natives grew in an, "Indian garden with melons, maize and beans, and to our surprise, a field of cotton." Today's farmers use about 10 canals that irrigate 33,000 acres of land growing corn, alfalfa, barley, wheat and cotton (see picture, above).

The latter is not just any cotton, but elegant Pima cotton – the best in the world. Though Pima cotton has its roots in Egypt, cotton's been around the area for centuries. A Salado storage basket in the Graham County Historical Society Museum, dated between A.D. 1200 to 1400, contains sandals and a torn swatch of cotton material dyed blue.

Pima Indians cultivated the plant on USDA experimental farms in the town of Sacaton, Arizona. The prized cotton, named for this tribe, was not unfamiliar to the Pimas. A report from Andrew Gray, a US Surveyor under the Treaty of Guadalupe Hidalgo wrote about his surveying expedition of the newly acquired land and described "...the rudely cultivated fields of the Pimas and Maricopas" growing "...cotton of the most superior kind. Its nature is not unlike that of the celebrated Sea Island cotton, possessing an equally fine texture, and, if anything, more of a silky fibre."

One thing that hasn't changed with the Gila Valley farmers down the decades is the place where they used to casually meet to shoot the breeze and learn the local buzz – Bush & Shurtz's. Once a hardware store in Thatcher, Bush & Shurtz has evolved into a restaurant on Arizona's Salsa Trail.

"You could set your watch on the farmers coming by to talk at 10 a.m. and 2 p.m.," said Bill Allred, who currently owns the building. "All the kibitzing and cracker barrel politics was at its best."

The tradition continues. Monday through Saturday, from 1 to 3 p.m., local farmers file in for lunch at a group of reserved tables at the front of the dining area. If you happen to sit within earshot, you'll hear their take on everything from politics to marriage.

Angle Orchard Swift Trail, Mount Graham
928-428-1605; www.angleorchard.com

Andrew and Viola Angle started this family orchard on Mount Graham in 1922. Story goes a logger tossed a peach pit around the Ladybug Trail in the early 1900s. The pit sprouted and grew into a fruit-bearing tree. Andrew tasted the fruit, found it sweet and juicy-good, leased 12 acres of land from the United States Forest Service and planted an orchard. The Angles hand-carried buckets of water flowing in Jacobson Canyon to the orchard.

Over the years, the orchard grew and changed hands within the family. While an irrigation pump made tending the orchard easier, bears, storms, freezing weather and pests brought perilous moments. Still, the mountain's been good to the Angles and the orchard has produced extraordinary fruit. Today, Betty Angle Larson, the original owners' granddaughter, owns and operates the orchard. The orchard grows 10 different apples, peaches, pears and cherries. Peach season runs from early July through mid-August. Apple season starts September 1 and usually runs through October.

Vernon Dozier's Produce Stand
(928-687-1036) 84 Frontage Road, York (near milepost 395 on US 70)

Just down the road from Gimee's restaurant, you can pick up some fresh-grown produce at Vernon's help-yourself produce stand. Depending on the harvest, you can pick up squash, okra, garlic, onions, apples and pears; or grab a jar of pickled jalapeños and canned green chile peppers. This is all on the honor system. You just weigh the produce on the scale and leave your money.

The whole setup is a slice of country life at its simplest. The best part is you can help yourself to a double portion. If you want, you can set a spell on the couple of chairs next to the tables of produce on the front porch and watch as the cars go by on the Old West Highway. And that part is free.

Vernon Dozier

Fort Grant Road

From Safford, go south on US 191 about 34 miles and head west on I-10; go 8 miles to exit no. 340, Fort Grant Road and head north. All venues are on or near Fort Grant Road.

The Sulphur Springs Valley is known for its cornucopia-like produce. Locavores will hit pay dirt with a drive down Fort Grant Road. From late spring through early fall, orchard, farms, ranches and vineyards share their harvests. Below is a sample of what's waiting, and when.

Apple Annie's Orchard 2081 W. Hardy Rd. (520-384-2084; www.appleannies.com) Features several varieties of apples, peaches and Asian pears.

Apple Annie's Produce & Pumpkins 6405 W. Williams Road (520-384-4685; www.appleannies.com). A farmer's market in its own right.

The Berry Farm 11515 N. Old Fort Grant Rd. (520-300-0337) Pesticide- and chemical-free boysenberries late May to early July.

Briggs & Eggers Orchard 17 miles north on Fort Grant Rd. (520-384-2539) Quality certified organic fruit.

Brown's Orchard 5774 N. Atwood Dr. (520-384-3671; www.youpickapples.com). Apples, pears and fed lamb.

Cook Family Cherry Orchard 7304 W. Ranch House Rd. (520-384-5849) Bing, Rainier and Brooks cherries.

Crop Circle Winery 3052 N. Fort Grant Rd. (520-384-3022) White and Red Merlot, Chardonnay and Syrah.

Valley Farms Ltd. Desert Sweet Organic 17 ½ miles north on Fort Grant Rd. (520-384-2861) Certified organic cherries and apples.

Photos this page: From top, (1) Sheep grazing in Sulphur Springs Valley, (2) Bob Bolinger from the Farmer's Club Opposite Page: from top, (1) Chef Terry Dagnino from Apache Gold Resort's Apache Grill, (2) Eurofresh Farms' packing operations (3) Panorama, one of many Eurofresh Farms' greenhouses; (inset) David Leitch with Eurofresh super tomatoes

Along the Salsa Trail - Real Arizona

Eurofresh Farms – One Hot Tomato
www.eurofresh.com
Not open to the public

You wouldn't necessarily connect an ordinary tomato farm with a brawny boiler room, Zwart Techniek generators that supply a megawatt of energy, or Hoogendoorn and Priva automated sensor boxes monitoring machines like a guardian angel would its wards. But then, Eurofresh Farms does not produce ordinary tomatoes.

Eurofresh began with the clichéd, yet axiomatic, advice of Ruth Stafford Peale – Find a need and fill it. Johan van den Berg found the need while on vacation in Pennsylvania during the holidays in the late 1980s. All the winter-weary produce on the store shelves started to appeal to his business sense. Johan and business partner Wil van Heyningen decided to fill the need for year-round good-tasting tomatoes in the U.S. and started Eurofresh Farms in 1990.

The third-generation Dutch greenhouse owners filled the need so well Euro-fresh Farms tomatoes developed a prestigious following (this would include

Salsa Fiesta, on Arizona's Salsa Trail). The tomatoes not only appear in the kitchens of the nation's finest chefs, the perfected red-orange globes consistently win ChefsBest™ awards as America's best-tasting tomato. Tomato greatness happens at Eurofresh Farms because nothing at Eurofresh Farms happens by accident.

David Leitch, general manager of packhouse operations, knows how much time, space and attention Eurofresh's tomato plants need to produce roughly 200 million pounds of tomatoes each year. And they're all grown on the vine, hydroponically and without pesticides.

"Eurofresh is innovative in the industry," said David. "The company invests in everything that is new."

The largest single-site glass operation in the United States is scientific and self-sustained. A boiler room powered by natural gas effuses enough carbon dioxide into each greenhouse to coax the plants to their fullest growing. Vats of highly refined fertilizer supply nutrients

Along the Salsa Trail - Destinations

117

to the plants' water. Hoogendoorn and Priva "sensor boxes" measure light, temperature and humidity and constantly feed this information to a main computer to assure everything stays copacetic. Zwart Techniek diesel generators stand by to power the site should the electricity fail. Even the bees that pollinate the plants do not come by accident.

"We use hive boxes full of bumblebees," David said, "because these bees are more efficient. If they do get outdoors, they don't communicate where they've

*Photos this page: A display of Eurofresh Farms products; **Opposite page:** from top, (1) One of two powerful Zwart Techniek diesel backup generators in case of power failure, (2) tomato vines growing in hydroponic nutrients, (3) Eurofresh Farms' boiler room*

been gathering pollen and they actually come back to the hive box. Also, they fit in the flower the most efficiently without damaging the blossom."

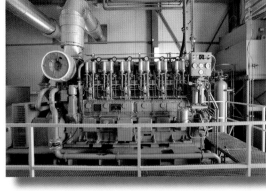

The whole goal of all this cutting-edge technology is to grow the most consistently excellent tomatoes year-round – Roma (best for cooking), Beefsteak (perfect to slap on a sandwich), Grape (bite-sized and sweet, for snacking), Campari (the sweetest) and Tomatoes on the Vine (Brilliant, all purpose).

Each tomato vine coils up an appointed string that controls their height. The vines, neatly aligned in long rows, grow up to 65 feet long and will produce every couple weeks for a whole year. Employees scrutinize every aspect of the plant's health and output. They balance plant height, pinch off sucker stems, prune extra flowers and leaves, pluck fruit and lower the plant so its spent portions look like ribbon candy to start the harvest cycle over again.

Most field-grown tomatoes are harvested when stone green, and then ripened via ethylene gas. This process produces a mealy texture and doesn't allow the taste and richness of the fruit to develop. Eurofresh tomatoes, on the other hand, get harvested when they reach a number 9 or 10 on the tomato ripeness color scale range of 1 to 12. The photosynthesis produces a sweeter tomato. Next, David revealed why tomatoes are best left on the vine when harvested.

"A tomato is basically a great tasting sack of water," David elucidated. "When it's picked fresh and ripe without a calyx (the whorl of green sepals at the end of the stem), the fruit lasts about a week. With a calyx, it'll last another three to four days. On the vine, the tomatoes will last two to three weeks. The king fruit, the one next to the cut, is the first to ripen and is usually the biggest."

In the final analysis, all this specialized science, serious research and pioneering technology add up to one thing – the making of one hot tomato.

Bonita Bean Co.
(520-384-2811) 7750 S. Kansas Settlement Road, Willcox

When it comes to pinto beans, you might say the West was won with this magical fruit. Well, at least these parts around Arizona's Salsa Trail. The beige bean

seed with the ruddy spots that inspired its name (pinto means painted in Spanish) repeatedly appeared, often solo, on pioneer plates and in cowboy chow. The pinto, and a good dose of intestinal fortitude, kept the human engine stoked.

Though beans landed on those penny-poor pioneer diets by default rather than choice, yesterday's humble pinto is today's most highly consumed bean in the U.S. Turns out the queen of beans is actually good for you, too. The pinto bean has a long list of health benefits – it's fat-free, packed with vitamins, high in fiber and helps prevent heart disease. George Mateljan, who started the nation's first healthy convenience food company, traveled the world to research the planet's healthiest foods. The namesake nonprofit foundation lists the pinto bean among the world's healthiest foods.

So our lowly pinto, which made the cowboy and pioneer meal go a long way as a bean for the means, has come a long way in image. A bean of means, you might say.

Since the Southwest is the nation's pinto bean basket, you can imagine how busy Bonita Bean Co. gets processing seven million of pounds of locally grown pinto beans each year. They ship them to Food City and Basha's grocery stores around Arizona and to distributors in California, Texas and Mexico, not to mention some of the restaurants on Arizona's Salsa Trail.

The bags of beans that leave this factory make some mean batches of beans. Not mean, as in low-class, nor mean as in average. But mean, as in b-a-d; which, according to *The Oxford English Dictionary*, means good, even excellent.

You see, the older the bean, the tougher it becomes and the longer it takes to cook, which can be bad (bad, as in not good). You can tell how fresh a bean is by its color: The fresher the bean, the lighter its color. As the dried pintos age, they become darker and tougher. Cooking time can double.

All the beans that leave the Bonita Bean Co. are all less than a year old. Some people say Bonita Beans are the best beans around. They sure are some of the freshest. And that's b-a-d.

Go south on US 191 about 34 miles and head west on I-10; go 8 miles to Exit 344; follow the signs to the vineyard.

"Wine has opened up a whole new avenue of life," said Jacque Cook (right), manager and part owner of Coronado Vineyards. "I get so much pleasure working here. The diversity of people that come here has opened my world."

Jacque's love for the vine started in Argentina. She and her husband, Mark Cook, lived there in the late 1990s when he contracted to plant the country's first pistachio orchards. Mark's family owns pistachio orchards near Arizona's Salsa Trail, and Mark grows chiles, garlic and a cherry orchard in Bowie, about 20 miles east of the vineyard.

While in Argentina, the Cooks became friends with an English teacher named Mariella Guiterriez whose father at that time was the Secretary to the Argentine government for the wine industry. As they toured the local wineries in the San Juan area with him, Jacque fell in love with the entire wine industry.

"I began dreaming of someday owning my own winery using Arizona wine grapes," Jacque said. "In 2005 we were approached by our friends who grow wine grapes here in Arizona to create this project."

The Cooks' friends owned what used to be the Yucca Sierra golf course and clubhouse, which is now home to Coronado Vineyards. The building was built in the early 1960's and abandoned in the early 1980s. The Cooks and their friends renovated the clubhouse in 2005 to make the tasting room, gift shop and restaurant/catering facilities. They planted the onsite vineyard in 2006.

"Mark and I now manage the winery, tasting room and onsite vineyard," Jacque

summed up her story, "while our partners grow all the grapes used for our wine production. My hope and dreams are for people to be able to blend their own wine here. We would ferment the grapes in barrels onsite and people would blend and label."

Oenophiles can sip Coronado's blends (left) at the wine tasting bar on the patio that looks at the Dos Cabezas Mountains or with Tuesday through Saturday lunch or Friday night dinner.

Along the Salsa Trail - Destinations

121

Farmer's Markets

Safford - *Graham County Chamber of Commerce Rest Area (1111 Thatcher Boulevard), from Mid-May to the end of September, Tuesday: 9 a.m. to Noon, Wednesday 2 p.m. to 5 p.m. and Saturday 8 a.m. to 1 p.m. (928-428-2511)*

Duncan – *The shady lot next to the post office (209 Main Street) and adjacent to Doc Lovett Park, Saturday 8 am to 11 am from mid-August to end of harvest (928-359-3590)*

At the Safford Farmer's Market, produce spreads across several tables, most everything "picked this morning." Orchard produce – apples, figs and pecans appear in their season. A chile vendor sells bags of arbol chiles, his hand-cranked grinder at his side to mill them for customers. Fresh eggs from free-range chickens go fast. The chile pepper roasters, available in several sizes, especially become popular during the chile pepper harvest in late summer. One of the grills keeps in constant motion roasting batches of peppers that perfume the air.

"I'm going to be a chile pepper and tomato freak next year," said Bill Cook, a visiting farmer from Duncan.

Duncan, located about 36 miles down US 70 just started its Farmer's Market in 2008. Bill recently moved to Duncan from a tiny town in the Verde River valley "because it was getting too crowded." Bill helped organize Duncan's farmer's market.

"I think our Farmer's Market is going to be a really sweet one," Bill said, "with lots of live music, kids performing, things like that. The high school ag teacher is also really involved in planning it."

Bill and Dan Rose traded farmer talk at Dan's booth as he cleaned scallions from his garden. Talk drifted from the tomato crops (there's been better years) to scallions (they're great). The owner of Arizona Desert Mesquite in Pima and local farmer by avocation sells mesquite rolling pins for making the perfect tortilla.

In an area of the state known for its agrarian abundance, you never know what you might find at the farmer's markets. One thing is for certain: If you want to be sure to find everything available, you best get there early.

Photos this page: from top, (1) a booth at Safford's Farmers Market (2) Dan Rose, (3) & (4) Fresh produce at Safford's Farmers Market, Opposite page, from top (1) Panorama of Discovery Park Campus with Mt. Graham in the background, (2) 20-inch Cassegrain reflector telescope, (3) Hubble deep space photograph

Museums & Tours

History and culture are alive and well on Arizona's Salsa Trail. Relics from native peoples from the ancients to the Apache, lore of mystical souls, routes of the Spanish conquistadors, stories of Mexican farmers and ranchers, colorful mining tales, vignettes about cowboys, Chinese sojourners, steely outlaws and Mormon chronicles make for some fascinating fodder. Add some cutting-edge space technology and natural history and you might say Arizona's Salsa Trail covers the gamut of human, spiritual and scientific interests.

Safford Area

Discovery Park
(928-428-6260) 1651 W. Discovery Park Boulevard, Safford

Like a mini-Epcot Center, Discovery Park started as a repository of information on the Southwest featuring biology, astronomy, ecology and physics. Now run by the University of Arizona, Discovery Park has evolved into a learning center. With

its Origins of the Universe gallery, monthly skywatch program, telescopes and unique box camera (one of the world's largest), the public can come and learn about this corner of the planet and the skies above it. Stargazing happens every Saturday night when weather permits, using a telescope once mounted in the observatory on Kitt Peak, just west of Tucson, and during star parties hosted by the Desert Stargazer Astronomy Club.

"We look at everyone's favorites," Dr. Swanson said about the skywatching program. "Saturn, Andromeda, the moon, Jupiter, double stars and star clusters. Young kids really get excited."

During the day, visitors can explore the park's terrestrial habitats and the wildlife they harbor, especially at the viewing ponds so attractive to migrating waterfowl. You might watch an avian drama unfold as a wintertime visiting merganser floats nonchalantly upon the mirrored surface of the viewing pond while a Cooper's hawk monitors the duck's every movement.

"Five species of hawks have been sighted on the grounds," Dr. Swanson reported.

The attractive natural landscape comes by way of hard work and dedication. Volunteers removed a tangle of tamarisk trees by hand to restore the 125 acres to a natural habitat of cottonwood, hackberry, desert broom, salt brush and willows. This restoration was recognized at the National Wetlands Awards in Washington, D.C. The landscape contains features akin to backcountry wetlands, country lanes (left), parks and open meadows.

Discovery Park has special tours of the habitat for students. The kids have the opportunity to learn about animal homes, animal tracks, tree rings, skulls and archaeology.

"People come back and tell us how connected they felt when they experienced Discovery Park and its programs as kids," said Dr. Swanson, "and then they bring their kids back. They like to share their interests."

Mount Graham International Observatory
928-428-6260 Tours depart from Discovery Park from mid-May through mid-November

"Up here it's all business," said John Ratje, site manager for Mt. Graham International Observatory. "It's no resort. The astronomers bring their own food, clean up after themselves, sleep on the second floor during the day and work all night."

Life inside the 16-story-high mountaintop observatory (right) operates on a different schedule and communicates with an esoteric lexicon. Here, miles are measured in light years, distance dissolves into infinity and time is of the essence. In the abstract world of the astronomer where thought takes precedence over action, the willingness to tend to the mundane duties of life is a testament to just how prestigious a rendezvous with the universe is these days at the Mt. Graham International Observatory.

This cachet comes from the unveiling of the observatory's new Large Binocular Telescope (LBT), the world's largest and most powerful (opposite page), located on one of the best observation points on the planet, 10,720-foot-high Mt. Graham. A consortium of partners from around the world built the $84 million telescope, sharing in its cost: The University of Arizona, Italy, Germany,

The Ohio State University and Research Corporation. Astronomers associated with these partners get first crack at observing the universe through the LBT. The one-acre observatory also has the Heinrich Hertz Submillimeter Telescope from which researchers study radio waves and the Vatican Advanced Technology Telescope.

Mt. Graham, with its dark, dry, transparent desert skies, fulfills all the atmospheric and low light requirements for a world-class observatory site. As a sky island that juts up out of the desert very quickly, the air flows around it more smoothly. This makes for better observations.

"Air bubbles in the atmosphere are like lenses in eyeglasses," Ratje explained. "The smoother the airflow, the less the turbulence in the air. On a good, dark night, the sky is extraordinary."

The LBT's unique binocular design has the light-gathering power of a single 39-foot mirror with a combined focus 10 times sharper than the Hubble Space Scope. The telescope's two giant spin-cast mirrors, made at the University of Arizona Mirror Lab, make the difference.

Honeycombed for stability and temperature control, the mirrors each weigh 18 tons and measure 28 feet across. The ability to control the mirrors' temperature removes the "twinkle factor" by taming the turbulence in the air bubbles in the atmosphere. The mirrors are polished to an accuracy of more than

25 nanometers, or 1/2000 the thickness of a human hair for an incomparably sharp image. The aluminum coating on the front of each mirror, about 100 atoms thick and equal to the amount of metal in a soda can, collects and concentrates light.

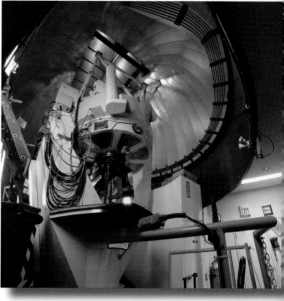

"Playing with light," Ratje mused. "That's what astronomy is all about."

The mirrors can be positioned to remove the light from stars and intensify the light from distant planets. This light manipulation, called constructive and destructive interference, allows astronomers to delve deeper into space, crack more interstellar mysteries and maybe even find non-terrestrial life forms.

"Some call this telescope a thing of beauty," Ratje said with understandable admiration, and then added wryly, "Some engineers call it a mechanical nightmare." (See photo left.)

The LBT's innovative design causes some head-scratching moments. For instance, in order to remedy maneuvering problems, engineers designed the top 10 stories of the observatory to move with the telescope. The optical support moves on two giant C-shaped rings. Ratje calls the LBT "a work in progress" because there will always be instrumentation to deal with. And while beauty certainly is in the eyes of the beholder, looking at the size and complexity of the LBT has an awesome effect not unlike the distances of objects and time frames of events in the universe.

Far too sophisticated for an astronomer to learn how to operate in a couple days, or even a week, the LBT requires a special operator. Like the captain of a 600-ton ship, the astronomer tells the operator where he or she want to go in the universe and the operator takes the astronomer there to within one arc second (1/3600 of a degree). If all goes well and the universe substantiates what the astronomer has calculated, the abstract theory becomes a reality, the findings gets memorialized in a scientific report and the astronomer gets the kudos. If not, the astronomer may have a long wait to get another night of face time with the LBT.

"This is the finest urban museum you'll ever see," said manager Mel Jones about the museum's historic building packed with relics, antiques, collectibles and colorful stories about the area and its cultures. "It makes a perfect museum setting from the creaking wooden floors to the large rooms. There's 15 in all." The large rooms, once classrooms in the Thatcher High School building built in 1917, hold a collection of stuff that gives invaluable insight to the area's cultural importance and traditions. Artfully arranged by subject or era, the rooms take you through hundreds of years of Gila Valley history using authentic antiques and memorabilia. Every object once held a special place in a Gila Valley household or business. Many are handmade and some are fascinating "firsts," such as the Edison TV.

"We're like the community depository," Jones explained how the museum came to own such an extraordinary collection. "We exist because people bring us their 'things.' Everything is local, and everything is free."

The Main Street display comprises a handful of smaller rooms that depict life as it might have looked. The rooms display relics from the old Valley National Bank (now owned by Chase Bank), a sheriff's office, the Graham Guardian newspaper and Dos Pobres Copper Mine just across the Gila River north of Safford.

"We used 100-plus-years-old barn wood to make the displays," Jones informed.

The Music Room has some of the first instruments played in the Valley. And since the Gila Valley Pioneers loved their music, the room is packed. The Russ Murdock Room, which Jones described as "a mini-museum in a mu-

Ladies white pleated cotton waist.
Donated by Berdes Frontz

Riding skirt from 1890's. Was worn by Kate Wanslee Jennings when she came here in the early 1900's.
Donated by Curtis A. Jennings

A riding skirt, circa 1890, worn by Kate Wanslee Jennings when she arrived in Safford in the early 1900's

an impressive collection of Native American artifacts. and next door is the Betty Murdock Doll Display showing off Russ' wife's hobby. The School and Fossil Room displays dinosaur

fossils and a native people's pottery display (above), and the Harvel H. Cosper Collection an impressive repository of Native American pottery and artifacts. In the Emerging Technology Room you can check out the first switchboard used in the county or send a telegram. The Vintage Clothing Room reviews styles and fashion, (right) and the Farm and Ranch Room features tools and implements of many different trades besides its namesakes.

The Courtroom and Office gives you a look into Judge Richard Chambers' "chambers."

If the rooms and all the items they hold don't ignite a bit of amazement, hearing the stories about the items will. Mel Jones, like the museum, is a repository of information. If he's around when you visit, he'll gladly give a free tour. After one of Jones' personal tours of the museum, you'll agree with the saying, The best things in life are free.

The Mills Collection
(928-428-8320) Eastern Arizona College, 615 N. Stadium Avenue, Thatcher

The archaeologically-rich Southwest has several areas and cultures that attract attention – the intriguing Trail of the Ancients that winds from Monument Valley northward to several sites in southeast Utah, mysterious Mesa Verde, powerful Casa Grande and enchanting Chaco Canyon. These glamorous spots had no trouble drawing archeologists to study them.

Photos opposite page: from top, (1) Lobby of the Student Services Building which houses the Mills Collection, including pottery, basketry, crotals and on page 126 examples of shell, (2) and (3) fine examples of Solado pottery

The Gila Valley, once part of the forbidding Apache lands called Apacheria, never really attracted much attention from archaeologists. Scientists knew the basin held a puzzling compendium of cultural remnants with elements from Hohokam, Mogollon, Anasazi and Mimbres cultures, but none knew why these native peoples gathered in the Safford Basin.

"This area is covered with archaeological sites," said Linda Blan, Anthropology Instructor at Eastern Arizona College in Thatcher. "It was a melting pot of Native American cultures. There was a pan-Southwestern abandonment going on in several culture areas. Large cultural systems were breaking down during a great drought, and some of the peoples from these different cultures ended up here in the Safford Basin."

Archaeologists call it The Area Between. It's a forgotten area that sits in the shadows of two monumental cultures: the ancient Mimbres in New Mexico whose artisans presented their supernatural world through exquisite black and white pottery and the engineering Hohokam who mastered farming in the central deserts around Phoenix and Casa Grande with canals and the art of recreation with ball fields.

The Area Between, unplumbed by the experts, became a well-known treasure field to area ranchers and farmers who found pottery, tools, metates and arrowheads when they worked their land. Some developed their hobby into an avocation. The Graham County Historical Society Museum has fine displays of some of these finds.

The most prolific of collectors was the husband and wife team, Jack and Vera Mills. The Mills excavated private land sites for 30 years, keeping notes, maps, drawings and published reports of their findings. The Mills unearthed more then 5,000 artifacts and 600 whole and restored pots.

"They did a good job for their time," said Blan. "They kept good records."

In the 1970s, the Mills collection was valued at more than $200,000 and attracted the attention of museums around the country as well as private and foreign investors. The Mills wished to keep the collection intact and displayed locally, however. Knowing this, the Eastern Arizona College's anthropology instructor at the time, Betty Lee, suggested the Mills consider the college.

After extensive negotiations, the college's EAC Foundation acquired the Jack and Vera Mills Collection. One of the terms of the purchase agreement requires the college to keep the collection on display in perpetuity. Blan manages the collection.

"This building," Blan said of the Student Services Building where the collection is displayed, "was designed around the collection."

Built-in cabinets and freestanding display cases show off artifacts, pottery and ceremonial objects. Some of the more unusual items include ancient Paleo Indian projectile points, Cloud Blowers for smoking, utilitarian Plain Ware and unique and colorful effigy pottery. The display has one of the largest collections of shell in the Southwest.

Besides its exquisite pottery, this world-class collection includes basketry, jewelry and crotals (copper bells). The collection also has some whimsy. One piece of pottery, Blan's favorite, is painted with what looks like curled cat tails.

"Who knows what the artist had in mind when he created the piece," Blan commented with a smile.

Jerry Berg's Woodcarvers Miniature World
(928-485-2484) 127 E. US 70, Pima

Jerry Berg's museum actually started 40 years ago when he visited the National Museum of Woodcarving in Custer, South Dakota. The model train aficionado was mesmerized by an exhibit created by Dr. Harley Niblack, who has since passed away, of animated caricature woodcarvings. Dr. Niblack had such a distinctive style and talent the Smithsonian Institute displayed three of his Western scenes currently in the South Dakota museum.

Left, *Jerry Berg at work*

"He was an amazing person," Jerry Berg said of Dr. Niblack, who worked with Walt Disney on animation projects. "You might say I thought I would do the same thing – create a woodcarving and make it move."

Though the good doctor didn't know it, he'd actually helped Jerry with his goal. Jerry studied the carvings and got the inspiration to, shall we say, carve his own journey in the world of miniature woodcarvings. Jerry admits his first carving was "crude." But, whittle by whittle, Jerry created his wild and wonderful Western world of animated miniature woodcarvings. But you don't have to be a kid to experience the same level of attraction Jerry did when he first saw animate carvings.

"I'd say kids from 2 years old to 100 are totally fascinated with the place," Jerry said. "Everyone that comes here really does enjoy it. And that makes every whittle worth it."

Like Dr. Niblack, Jerry focuses on Western motifs and characters. He paints them with primary colors, heavy on red and yellow, which gives the scenes a rollicking look. Jerry specializes in facial expressions. The big mouths and teeth he carves on characters give them rubber faces. Dr. Niblack used dental tools for his carving, but Jerry uses classic carving tools, joking that he married his wife Karen (also a woodcarver who displays her exquisite bird pieces in the museum) for her woodcarving tools. After four decades, Jerry estimated it takes him only five hours to create a character compared to several weeks when he first started.

"I originally named them," Jerry admitted about his burgeoning collection of carvings, which fills 2,000 square feet, "but after 3,000, who can keep up?"

Although 3,000 pieces may seem obsessive, Dr. Niblack created around 70,000 pieces. With that in mind, Jerry has a long way to go.

Rex Allen Arizona Cowboy Museum
(520-384-4583) 150 N. Railroad Avenue, Willcox

Five-year-old Elvie Allen already knew how to ride a horse when his family moved to Willcox. Cross-eyed and shy, Elvie had a long way to go before he'd become famous and known as The Arizona Cowboy.

Elvie had innate musical talent, taking after his dad, Horace, who played the violin by ear. Horace gave Elvie a guitar from Sears when he turned 11. Elvie taught himself chords and could play well enough to accompany his dad on stage. When Elvie's voice turned from tenor to baritone, people started listening. What Elvie lacked in his eyesight was made up in his voice.

"God gave me a good voice," said the late Elvie Rex Allen, later known as Rex Allen, "and that voice has been good to me."

That voice got him a radio slot on WLS Radio in Chicago, whose announcer liked the fact this "Arizona Cowboy is a genuine cowboy from Arizona." Then it got him on records, into the movies and on TV. When Rex teamed up with his horse, Koko, the duo became cinema heroes. Along the way, Rex's eyesight was corrected. The Lions Club paid for an operation to help fix Elvie's eyes back in Willcox, but it would take more surgery down the road to eventually correct the problem.

Brushing all stardust aside, Rex never forgot about the town in which he grew up (nor the Lions Club). He often returned to Willcox, and he helped start his namesake museum. Pierre Brehm – an Arizona Ranger, Willcox's Official Tour Guide and a familiar face around the museum – will tell you all about his friend Rex and share anecdotes about him as well as history, in general, of the area. If you have time, Pierre will give you a free tour of the town.

"Rex had a memory that would put an elephant to shame," octogenarian Pierre, no slouch in the memory department himself, recalled. "He remembered his fans and the people he worked with."

The museum is packed with memorabilia, photographs and stories – the best accounts being recollections from Pierre. Browse the museum then sit yourself down right where the big Rex used to sit and let Pierre fill you in on the rest of the story about the tenderhearted cowboy who, Pierre said, "kept alive the true spirit of the Arizona West."

Clifton Area

Greenlee County Historical Society Museum
(928-865-3115) 315 Chase Creek, Clifton

Here's to Arizona
The Fairest Daughter of the sun
Whose veins are of silver
With sinews of copper
And a heart of gold

Some small town museums are like your grandmother's attic, a little disorganized but packed with interesting, albeit esoteric stuff. Some act like over-protective parents with cordoned off displays monitored by curators and ever-watchful docents. Greenlee County Historical Society Museum is unlike your grandmother's home – neat and tidy with some pretty interesting stuff. This would be the eccentric grandmother's home without the lace doilies and formal parlor we're talking about. This is the one that saw a lot of color in her life but was softhearted enough to save her keepsakes.

If you take a spin around Clifton, you'd quickly understand a lot of money once passed through this multi-cultural town. The high life happened in Clifton's yesteryears and the historical society museum is the repository of its relics.

You'll find a lot of interesting items and information from  those mining days when lifestyles teetered between oysters on the half-shell and rotgut whiskey. These are things garnered from exquisite homes and everyday businesses: art pieces with names like De Grazia and Parrish; hardware like century-old old miner's lanterns and inventions like the Graphophone;  dozens of old photographs that have fascinating stories; and pieces of a lawyer's entertainment room wall with graffiti drawn by guests from around the world that tells some rather unique tales:

Did you ever hear of "Captain Wattle"
He was all for love and
A little for the Bottle.

Getting back to the museum being more like a grandmother's house, it does have a hefty collection of old-time domestic items, circa your great-grandmother's era. Where else would you find the high chair U.S. Supreme Court Justice Sandra Day O'Connor sat in? Or the registry of graves in the Mexican Cemetery just north of Morenci on the east side of US 191? Remember, this is the eccentric grandmother.

When you're done perusing, don't forget to take a look at their pint-sized gift shop. They have some great deals on silver and turquoise jewelry and books.

Each of the nation's precious metals has an association with a Western state: California earned the nickname of Gold Mountain during its Gold Rush days. Nevada boasts it is The Silver State on its license plates. Arizona is the Copper King. And the king of the North American copper mines is Freeport-McMoRan Copper & Gold, Inc.'s Morenci copper mine.

Copper has shown up around the world throughout the millennia, maybe as early as 10,000 B.C. The malleable and highly conductible metal has been used in tools and technology by ancient peoples to astronauts. Culturally, copper shows up as the ankh in ancient Egypt, the Greek's *chalkos* and the star in Arizona's flag.

Arizona's cache of copper came by volcanism, which created a mass of deposits that runs from one end of the state to the other. In Clifton and Morenci, early copper miners could easily collect rich returns from deposits located in cliffs.

As the surface copper played out, miners had to dig deeper to glean 100 to 200 pounds of metal per ton of ore.

Today's Morenci Copper Mine produces about five pounds of copper per ton of ore from three open pits. Trucks with tires almost 12 feet in diameter carry loads of 270 tons of ore. The copper gets eventually extracted through an electrowinnowing process with "zero-discharge."

The Morenci Mine's story started, like many other mining camps in the area, when the Apaches formally agreed to give up the fight. With the peace pact ink barely dried from the treaty table and the 1872 Mining Act freshly in place, prospectors decided to take a

Photos opposite page: from top, *(1) Don Lunt sits next to retired Supreme Court Justice Sandra Day O'Connor's highchair (2) Carbide mining lamps, (3) Cartoon Map by the artist Hal Empie, circa 1950.* *This page:* Ore hauler dwarfs visitors on a mine tour.

second look at Henry Clifton's discovery eight years earlier of a rich malachite deposit in the walls of Chase Creek canyon. Clifton, fearing for his life because of the Apaches, had never developed the deposit.

Still wild and stained with occasional bloody skirmishes, the land soon buzzed with prospectors and miners. Locating the mineral deposits was the easy part. One prospector, Colonel Del Potter, formerly an Indian scout

with the Cavalry, discovered more than 600 mines, many of them gold. Creating worthwhile profit margins from copper deposits took ingenuity, elbow grease and money.

Robert Metcalf and his brother owned one of the more productive copper mines called the Longfellow Mine. They ended up appealing to New Mexico acquaintance Charles Lesinsky for investment monies and eventually

sold out to Lesinsky and his brother. The Lesinskys got tired of shipping the ore to Swansea, Wales for smelting and built a one-ton adobe smelter of their own on Chase Creek along with a baby gauge railroad from the mine to the smelter. The first year, the trip took 30 minutes down, and two hours back up to the mine via burro. The next year Little Emma, the steam engine, came on board.

Though copper's had its ups and downs in the world market, the versatile mineral always recovers like a phoenix from the ashes. After the second Industrial Age sent nations clamoring for copper around the turn of the 20th century, the market crashed

Photos this page: from top, (1) Sheet of copper oxidized by exposure to air and chemicals; (2) group on tour examines electroplated copper sheet. Opposite Page, top: (1) Electrowinnowing facility, (3) Tour guide explains the plating process, Bottom: Tour visitors examine copper plates.

and prices dipped low enough to shut down several mines after World War II. An increased demand for copper and other metals from China, India and other industrialized nations has caused another boom in recent years.

With more than 700,000 tons of ore mined 24/7, you can understand how the pit mine, already three miles wide back in 1937, expanded enough by the 1960s to remove the town of Morenci from its place along Chase Creek. New Morenci, where you can hop on a morning or afternoon mine tour (reservations required), sits several switchbacks and several steep miles north of Clifton on US 191.

A tour supplies a ton of facts and figures regarding copper, such as today's average home has more than 400 pounds of the alloy and each person born will typically use about 1,500 pounds of copper in his or her lifetime. The tour provides an up-close look at the machines that make the mine run as well as some important cultural insights. You see, copper not only played an important role in the development of Arizona, but it actually had a hand in the genesis of Ari-

zona's Salsa Trail.

"Back in the early days, the mining company kept expanding and buying out the mines in the area," Julio Tavision, a former Morenci mine employee who now works as a Copper Guide, said. "As the need for employees grew, the mine reached into Mexico as far as Chihuahua to recruit workers. My father was part of a group from Chihuahua. That drew the large Hispanic population to eastern Arizona."

With the Hispanics came their culture and food. The rest, as they say, is Salsa Trail history.

No matter where you go along Arizona's Salsa Trail, we have birds. From flocks of yellow-winged black birds gleaning in the field of a roadside farm to a rare sighting of a yellow-billed cuckoo in a streamside cottonwood-willow riparian forest. Birds of all colors come our way, from tricolored herons to violet-green swallows in all seasons, from crimson-colored cardinals darting around the desert treetops in wintertime to vermilion flycatchers fidgeting on streamside branches in the summer. And all sizes are seen, from diminutive white-eared hummingbirds zooming around pine-oak forests to bald eagles gloriously gliding around waterways.

More than 300 species of birds have been recorded in Graham County, a region that had the highest species count during the Arizona Breeding Bird Atlas fieldwork studies. You may spot a life-lister right in town, around nearby lakes or ponds, inside canyons or atop the state's third highest mountain. When you check out our birding spots (pick up the *Graham County Arizona – A hidden treasure for birders!* brochure at the Graham County Chamber office) you'll understand what a hidden treasure Arizona's Salsa Trail is for birding. There is only one word to describe this experience . . .

Magnificent

BIRDING

BIRDING SIGHTS AROUND TOWN

Roper Lake State Park

From US 70, go south on US 191 about 5 miles to the park's signed turn-off, and turn left (east).

Roper Lake brings birdwatchers from around the world. Its aquatic and riparian woodland habitat has attracted a list of about 120 species. White and brown pelicans occasionally show up, and you may even catch sight of a least bittern or black-crowned night heron. State Park rangers and local birders post recent sightings on a list at the entry gate.

Cluff Ranch

Go west on US 70 to Pima, and turn left onto Main Street; turn left onto Cluff Ranch Road, a maintained dirt road, and take it to the ponds.

Cluff Ranch brings you to the foot of the Pinaleño Mountains where runoff drains into area ponds that attract a number of species of birds as well as other wildlife.

Photos: above, Yellow-headed Blackbirds in Safford field, below: Great Blue Heron at Roper Lake.

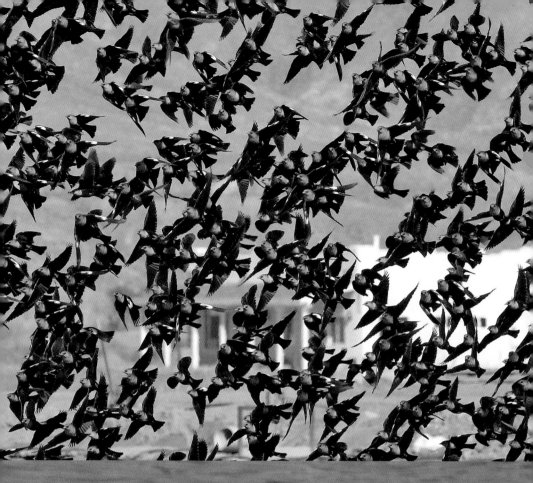

Discovery Park

From US 70, go south on 20th Avenue to the signed turnoff for the park.

Several different habitats give you a chance to see a variety of birds along short trails. Waterfowl, hawks, falcons, hummingbirds and a number of neotropical migrants visit the wetlands, riparian woodland and grasslands.

Reay Lane Reclamation Ponds & Marsh

Go east on US 70 to Thatcher, and turn right (north) onto Reay Lane; ponds are just below the river.

Here's where you get to see rare sightings right in town. The constructed wetlands of ponds and marshes make a great place for waterfowl and shorebirds.

BACKCOUNTRY SPOTS

The Gila River & Bonita Creek

To reach the west side from Safford: *Go 5 miles east*  *on US 70 to Solomon; turn left (north) onto Sanchez Road and follow the road to the end of the pavement; continue on the graded dirt road and follow the signs to Bonita Creek and the lower end of the Gila Box.* To reach the east side from Safford: *Go 10 miles east on US 70 to its junction with US 191 and turn left (north); go 29 miles to milepost 160 and turn left (west) onto the signed Black Hills Back Country Byway; follow the road 4 miles to the conservation area.*

Along the Gila River, you can catch waterfowl and shorebirds while hawks and eagles glide its skies. Keep an eye out for bighorn sheep, too.

One of the stars of the birdwatching show is Bonita Creek, where more than 140 species of birds  live or pass through the creek's canyon. More than 70 of these species nest right along the creek. Watch for the common blackhawk and zone-tailed hawk.

The Swift Trail

From US 70, go south on US 191 for 8 miles; turn right (west) at the signed turnoff for AZ366, the Swift Trail.

The Swift Trail, which takes you from the desert floor to sub-alpine meadows provides a rare chance to just about see it all – from cactus wrens to Clark's Nutcrackers, Harris' hawks to northern goshawks, burrowing owls to spotted owls. Waterfowl appear at Riggs Lake.

Haekel Road & Ponds

Go east on US 70 for 8 miles and turn right (south) onto Haekel Road.

Haekel Road takes you into the San Simon Valley where desert grasslands become an active winter habitat for hawks, buntings and sparrows. Travel 25 miles to the signed Hot Well Dunes for a look at the wetlands habitat formed from the hot springs.

Aravaipa Canyon and Turkey Creek

Go west on US 70 about 7 miles past Pima and turn left onto Klondyke Road; go 25 miles to Aravaipa Road and turn right (west); go 20 miles to the parking area for Aravaipa Canyon.

Aravaipa Creek and its riparian forest of cottonwood, willow, ash and syca-more trees is the big draw for the 230 species of birds sighted in its can-yon. Forests of saguaro cactuses cover streamside slopes. Wear footgear you don't mind getting wet, and watch for bighorn sheep and coatimundi.

Photos opposite page: from top, (1) Belted Kingfisher at Bonita Creek, (2) Pens-tomen, hummingbirds favorite nectar source, along the Swift Trail, (3) Ferruginous Hawk along Haekel Road, This Page: Serious birdwatchers, insert, Red Tailed Hawk in Sulphur Springs Valley. Background: Black-Crowned Night-Heron nearly disap-pears in the winter twilight at Cluff Ponds.

While Arizona's Salsa Trail keeps things cooking around town, it has a hidden side that's hotter than a habanero. Secreted away, in a subterranean process, flows a nepenthe for stress and disease.

Safford's aquifer holds geothermal fields. Here, water flows underground much like it does in streams and creeks, but at a much slower pace. In an aquifer, water percolates in between grains of sand, gravel and rocks. In Safford's case, these solid elements contain hot rocks from volcanic activity that occurred 1.5 to 2 million years ago. These radiating relics heat the water and, like a hot air balloon, the water rises to the surface in the form of hot springs.

"This whole area is a result of volcanic activity," said David Morris, geology and astronomy instructor at Eastern Arizona College in Thatcher. "Most local mountain ranges, except for Mt. Graham, are made of lava rock. Mt. Graham is an exception. It's the exposed core of an old mountain range that has been uplifted."

Years ago, these hot springs drew "well seekers" to the area. Artist Hal Empie's father, Hart Dewitt Empie, arrived in Safford on a stretcher. The elder Empie lived into his 90s and, like father like son, so did Hal. Not everyone welcomed these hot springs.

In 1875, when homesteaders considered the worth of water for little more than utilitarian use, these hot springs were considered a nuisance. Especially since the Eighth Territorial Legislature had offered a $3,000 reward to the first person to locate artesian water anywhere in the state. The first find happened in the Sulphur Springs Valley at the southern end of Arizona's Salsa Trail. Graham County's "first" occurred six years later.

"It is regrettable to note, in retrospect," wrote local historian William Ryder Ridgway, who penned a column for the Graham County Courier of local interesting stories, "…the underground wells were too mineral-laden and not suitable for farming."

As the saying goes, one man's garbage is another's treasure. People still came to soak in the area's hot springs for their health, claiming relief from all kinds of ailments. One hot spring in Eden became infamous for its mix of health and hedonism.

Named for the native peoples who first soaked there, Indian Hot Springs evolved into a resort and showed a more glamorous, if not colorful, side of the area. The Mansion, as the turn of the 20th century accommodations were affectionately called, made it through the Roaring 20s, nudist hippies and raucous rock stars.

Many diverse groups visited the springs, from scout troops to families and corporate types to new age groups. Some say the resort was haunted.

"The hot springs at Eden were famous," said Morris. "There were stories about the Rolling Stones, Grateful Dead and even ghosts hanging out there. Everyone snuck into the place to go skinny dipping."

Over the years, Indian Hot Springs may have raised a few eyebrows but it soothed a lot of souls. Alas, the Mansion burned down recently, putting an end to its sensational saga.

Artesian springs bubble up all over the Valley, from primitive spots along the Gila and San Francisco rivers to developed al fresco pools to health spas featuring indoor private baths.

Essence of Tranquility (928-428-9312)
6074 Lebanon Loop, Safford

Almost 60 years ago, the hot mineral springs at the Essence of Tranquility gurgled indecorously into a mud puddle. The original owners called the springs "Lebanon" after the biblical Pools of Lebanon where an angel occasionally agitated the waters and the sick and lame could get healed if they got into the pool when the waters stirred. The springs have eventually graduated from a puddle to six separate pools ranging from 103 to 106 degrees. But they still, many say, hold the healing powers of the Pools of Lebanon.

"The water works because of faith," co-owner, Clarise Drake, said. "Also, the water has a lot of sodium, which draws out a lot of poisons and stress. Believe it or not, the water draws stresses out."

The spa's popularity, Drake added, not only comes from the water's health benefits, but the spa's "funkified" homey atmosphere consisting of plastic flowers and kitschy curios, decorative outside lights and cozy sitting areas scattered around the spa's grounds.

Kachina Hot Springs Mineral Spa
(928-428-7212) 1155 W. Cactus Road, Safford

Located at the base of Mt. Graham in an area called Artesia because of its many free-flowing hot springs, Kachina Mineral Springs bubbles with water from a hot thermal pool hovering around 108 degrees. The spa has several private mineral baths which pour in Roman-style tubs cleaned and scrubbed after each use. A large communal tub is also available

"The biggest reason people return for is the water makes them feel good," said manager Stella LaFerriere. "There's nothing like soaking in the water. Combined with a massage, it's the ultimate."

The secret of the spa's popular combination treatment – a 15-minute soak, foot reflexology massage, herbal sweat wrap and full-body massage – is in the hot springs.

"Artesian water is very soft," owner Joe Garzon explained. "It feels nice next to the skin. Also, it's high in calcium, fluoride and potassium; and it has traces of lithium. What happens is it relaxes the muscles and loosens things up so the masseuse can get deeper. The massage helps detoxify the body."

Hot Well Dunes Recreation Area
(928-348-4400) 25 miles south of US 70 off Haekel Road

Outdoors and surrounded by sand dunes, the Bureau of Land Management's Hot Well Dunes Recreation Area exists by accident. Drillers seeking oil instead hit a pocket of hot water 1,920 feet under the sand. Up gushed 106 degree water, which flows at 250 gallons per minute.

From its two outdoor tubs, soakers can view the rolling sand dunes and the jagged peaks of the Peloncillo Mountains in the distance. One tub sits in the shade of a giant tamarisk, the other basks in the sun. At night, bathers soak under a canopy of stars.

"A visit to the Hot Well Dunes Recreation Area is a great way to unwind," said Diane Drobka, public relations person with the BLM. "The mineral springs provide soothing therapy for aching muscles or simply a fun way to relax with friends. And, since you're surrounded by 2,000 acres of sand dunes, it's almost like a day at the beach."

Hot Springs *(Roper Lake State Park)*
(928-428-6760) 101 E. Roper Lake Road, Safford

The stone-lined mineral hot springs is a favorite among weary travelers who take to the outdoors. With body-temperature water to lull you down several notches on the de-stressor scale, the pool makes a grand finale for a day of birdwatching or hiking on the park's avian gathering grounds.

Mobu Herbals
(928-428-0704) mobuherbals.com
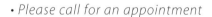

• Please call for an appointment

What started in Jannel Hendricks-Cole's home with her making lip balms has grown into a nationwide business of herbal balms for conditions that ailed her patients. A sign that reads: Warning: 100 Percent Natural explains why. Hendricks-Cole does on-site production of an exclusive line of herbal products she created. "These are herbal products that benefit people," said Hendricks-Cole, a naturopath and master herbalist. "There's a balm for pain, energy, infections, keeping regular and 35-plus balms for men and women."

When you contact Mobu Herbals, mention Arizona's Salsa Trail. When you do, you'll get a free Chili Mango Lip balm. They don't call Señor Salsa Hot Lips for nothing, you know.

Swift Trail Parkway
Like Traveling From Mexico to Canada

Directions: From US 70, go south on US 191 for 8 miles; turn right (west) at the signed turnoff for AZ 366, the Swift Trail. Milepost 22 to the top closed from November 15 to April 15 (or longer if snow persists).

When artist Hal Empie and three friends embarked on their expedition to the top of Mount Graham in the summer of 1925, they made sure they had enough to eat. Empie describes the group as *"western boys attuned to the fine art of over-preparation."* They loaded their pack mules with *"a gallon of tea garden syrup* [cane sugar syrup], *a case of pork and beans, a case of No. 2 canned tomatoes, Nabisco cookies, a carton of Hershey bars, 50 pounds of flour, a 25-pound can of lard, a whole ham, a whole side of bacon, flapjack flour"* and cumbersome frying pans, utensils and an iron skillet. After a rainstorm, encounters with black bears trying to purloin portions of their provisions (one of which got away with the ham and bacon) and fishing black bear style, the boys ran out of provisions after 15 days and made their way home.

Cascades along Ash Creek Trail

These days, traveling up Mt. Graham in the Pinaleño Mountains takes only a few hours there and back on the Swift Trail Parkway (first 22 miles paved, last 13.2 graded). The national al scenic byway starts on the desert floor at US 191 (3,200 feet) and coils up the most vertical rise in the state through five life zones, ending at 10,720 feet. The byway had many builders – pioneers, the forest service, Civilian Conservation Corps and Graham County. The name hon-

Ancient moss-covered Douglas Firs line the Ash Creek Trail along the way to the falls.

ors a former forest supervisor, Theodore T. Swift, who established the route.

Arizona's version of a coastal rain forest rises more than 6,000 feet and contains ancient Douglas fir trees. A Hudsonian-Boreal forest of mixed conifer and aspen trees at the end of the route makes the landscape look more Canadian than Sonoran Desert.

Western Wallflower visited by a Tiger Moth - Swift Trail

The mountain has an intensely rich

natural diversity due to its sky island status. Sky island mountain ranges rise rapidly from the desert floor. The group of sky islands in southeastern Arizona, called the Madrean Archipelago, vault just like a chain of islands only surrounded by grasslands and desert instead the sea. The archipelago is one of three megadiversity centers of the world. *The Pinaleño Mountains' diversity includes 18 different plants and animals found nowhere else on the planet.*

The natural wonders seen on Mt. Graham aren't tethered solely to terra firma. Some are not of this world. The Large Binocular Telescope Observatory, which houses Earth's largest telescope, is located upon the mountain (see page 120). This telescope studies the universe with more clarity than the Hubble Space Telescope.

Pick up a *Pinaleño Mountains Automobile Tour* brochure at the Graham County Chamber office for a list of destinations and mileages along the Swift Trail Parkway. The list includes side trips to picnic areas, far-reaching viewpoints, wildflower-filled meadows and fir-forest trails.

Right - Spectacular 200 foot Ash Creek waterfall viewed from the Ash Creek Trail.

Black Hills
Back Country Byway

Directions from: South end: Go about 10 miles east on US 70 to its junction with US 191 and turn left (north); go to the signed turnoff for the Byway at milepost 139 and turn left (north); North end: Continue on US 191 to milepost 160 and turn left (west). High clearance vehicle required.

With far-reaching views of scenery beautiful enough to si-

landscape became part of the Western and Chiricahua Apache people's historic territory. During Cochise's resistance, some Apaches used the land as a holdout.

In 1826, mountain man James O. Pattie trapped beaver along the Gila River, which the byway crosses at its northern end. Twenty years later, General Kearney and guide Kit Carson passed through the Gila Box, a handful of miles north of the byway. Cattlemen ranched the area and merchants

lence the most compulsive mind, the 21-mile-long Black Hills Back Country Byway feels too remote to attract the attention of civilization. The span of land the byway crosses in the northern Peloncillo Mountains, however, has had many brushes with humanity.

Francisco Vásquez de Coronado, in search of the golden Cities of Cibola, passed by here during his expedition in the 16th century. The Mogollon people farmed the area a thousand years ago, and then the

traveled across this land to deliver produce and wood to mines in Clifton. The Byway, originally called the Safford-Clifton Road, was built by prisoners from 1914 to 1920 to enhance this commerce.

You can see relics of the past right along the dirt road – from the grave of one of the prisoners who tried to escape during the road construction to cattle equipment and old mines to remnants from the Mogollon people. On the eastern end of the Byway, near milepost 16, look for remnants of a Civilian Conservation Camp built in the 1930s. Look for erosion barriers on the hillsides, a rectangular rock building where dynamite was stored, a sidewalk that led to a tent with rock mounds where flagpoles stood and low rockwalls demarcating the campgrounds.

Around milepost 17, check out a shady picnic area just under a patented double luten arch bridge (below) built in 1918 and take a walk along the Gila River.

One of the Byway's best features is the scenery of the Peloncillo Mountains. Covered with creosote bushes, yucca and an occasional juniper tree, the volcanic range contains attractive lava flows and tuff formations. The lava flows show dark gray and gray-brown rock. The tuff, or volcanic ash, looks light gray with red or yellow hues. This coloration creates stunning settings.

As a result of this volcanism, which took place 20 million years ago, the area has a rare occurrence of fire agates. Only found in parts of California, Arizona and Mexico, these ruddy semi-precious gemstones don't come easy. You might find a worthy specimen in the signed rockhound area on the road's southern end. No doubt you will find some interesting pieces of chalcedony to take home. The best part is the rocks are free and fun to find.

Opposite Page: from top, (1) near the western access to the Black Hills Back Country Byway, (2) Brick oven at the CCC camp (3) Moonrise over Black Hills.

San Francisco River
Scenic Drive

Directions: Go east on US 70 about 10 miles to its junction with U.S. US 191, and turn left (north); go about 48 miles to Clifton, and turn east (right) onto Frisco Avenue (just past the historic train depot).

Nicknamed by the locals the *Million Dollar Road That Goes to Nowhere*, this graded and well-engineered road takes you right along the San Francisco River. If the original plans were fulfilled, the road would have connected Clif-

The Million Dollar Road has priceless views

ton with the Blue River where an old settlement called Boyles once stood.

At the turn of the 20th century, many people homesteaded there at the confluence of the two rivers. Boyles even had a post office, store, saloon and a school that taught up to 40 children. Chinamen tilled small vegetable farms along the banks, and they sold their produce to the miners downriver in Clifton. But any trace of the farms and settlement has gone the way of the rivers.

The developed road disappears after only a few miles. Its abrupt end came by way of dollars – or lack of – rather than floods. Once the powers that be counted this road's costs, which tallied about $1 million a mile to build, construction stopped.

You can still travel the few miles on this scenic drive. As soon as you cross the bridge, a half-mile from the highway, and make your way past the trailer park, the backcountry takes over.

The Million Dollar Road That Goes to Nowhere ends, but the scenery doesn't. You can continue on foot all the way to the Blue River, but be ready to hike right in he river.

When the road ends, sightseers should return the way they came. Experienced hikers can continue to the Blue River and beyond. The further you travel up the river, the more surreal the scenery becomes – high canyon walls dip and heave tumultuously, copper patinas drip from mineral-rich pockets and fist-sized clusters of crystals glimmer from pocks in the rock walls. Also, the further you get upriver, the harder the waterway becomes to negotiate—segments of quicksand, labyrinthine willow thickets and tedious stretches of rock-hopping. If you feel comfortable in remote river canyons, the rough-and-tumble world of the San Francisco River will give you an unforgettable backcountry experience.

Kayaking after winter rains

If you plan to explore the river up close, always stay tuned to weather reports. Here along the "Frisco," life becomes contingent on the river's terms.

Above, November Gold and below, one of many spectacular panoramas along the San Francisco River

Chase Creek
Located just off US 191 in Clifton

*P*art Old World, a little ramshackle and certainly full of character, Chase Creek was once the pulse of Clifton. Originally called Copper Avenue, the townsfolk nicknamed the street Chase Creek after the dry wash gouged alongside it by constant floods.

Street life, back in the late 1800s, moved under a grey pallor of smoke that belched from a smelter. Caves hewn in cliffs behind several buildings secreted valuables, such as whiskey, or stored perishables like meat and vegetables. A blend of businesses kept the street busy with shoppers. In a mostly male town, this included bordellos, saloons and gambling rooms. Sacred Heart Catholic Church balanced the vice with virtue.

Chase Creek dry wash not only served as a natural drainage but it doubled as a corridor for cattle drives. Thousands of cattle traveled the slag-covered wash floor brushing against walls overlaid with tuff stone. The Western beef enjoyed

its moment in the limelight at the Mardi Gras celebration of 1899 in New Orleans, a city whose French Quarter streets could have been the pattern for Chase Creek.

Narrow, full of moody shadows and lined with historic buildings, Chase Creek begs to resurrect the memories of its heydays. You can check out its past in pictures and antiques at the Greenlee County Historical Society; take a walking tour to peruse the architectural work of master craftsmen, like Jose Salinas, who embellished Sacred Heart Catholic Church and the Palicio House with plaster reliefs; or imagine the raucous behavior that prevailed in the always-crowded hewn-out-of-the-cliff-walls-jail south of the historic railroad station.

Along the Salsa Trail - Real Arizona

An old Chevy (left) "still runs," says its owner, a gold prospector who lives on the outskirts of the town and advises you "can hardly pay for your gas with the gold you find here."

Stoneworker Margarito Varela carved the cliff face with a pick, drill and blaster to create the escape-proof and dungeon-like hoosegow. Brawny iron bars and doors kept the prisoners, many of the West's most nefarious bad men, in place. In an interesting twist of fate, Varela ended up the jail's first prisoner. The story goes he celebrated too raucously when he finished the project. When he fired his gun in Hovey's Dance Hall to announce the jail's completion, the proprietor, also the town sheriff, arrested Varela and threw him in the clink to cool off.

If you look up to the top of the cliff across and a little south from P.J.'s, called Mars Bluff, you can see a group of flags. If you take the half-mile hike up the hill, you come to a war memorial lined with flags and scattered with military dog tags. The memorial started out with dog tags from all the veterans in town—dead or alive—from each of the armed forces.
Word spread and now veterans from all over the nation visit Mars Bluff and add their dog tags to the monument. Townsfolk still talk about the big storm in the fall of 2007 that blew every flag down but the American flag and they thought that pretty special.

GREENLEE COUNTY HISTORICAL SOCIETY
THE EAGLES' HALL
HAS BEEN PLACED ON THE
NATIONAL REGISTER
OF HISTORIC PLACES
BY THE UNITED STATES
DEPARTMENT OF THE INTERIOR

Opposite page: historic buildings along Chase Creek. **This page: above,** *Rocky Mountain bighorn sheep are a common sight around Chase Creek,* **right,** *many of the buildings are listed on the National Register of Historic Places.*

155

Willcox Playa
A Wildlife Happening

Directions: *From Willcox, go 6 miles east on AZ 186 and turn south on Kansas Settlement Road; go 4 miles to the signed turnoff for the Willcox Playa Wildlife Area.*

The Willcox Playa, located in the middle of the mountain range-ringed Sulphur Springs Valley, lives up to its Spanish name playa, which means beach. Thousands of years ago, the waters of Lake Cochise lapped at this lowest point in the valley. Now the area looks like a dune-rumpled beach surrounding a dry lakebed white with alkali. The ancient bed transforms into a shallow wetland during the monsoons and in the winter when moisture from all those

surrounding mountains eventually drains into the playa. Snowbirds have taken particular note of this.

While most North American beaches are known for summertime fun, this one comes alive in the winter. From October into March, this playa becomes a wildlife happening when sandhill cranes migrate from the continent's

north country to the valley. Each year since scientists began to document the birds' arrival in 1948, the cranes have used the Willcox Playa as a major roosting spot during their stay. Over the years, the flock has grown from 750

birds logged in the first official Arizona Department of Game & fish survey to 36,418 counted in 2008.

The elegant bird with a folklore that portends long life and prosperity stands four to five feet high and has a seven-foot wingspan. Mostly grey with a red cap of skin upon its head, the leggy bird congregates and flies in patterns similar to another winter visitor, the Canada goose. The cranes sleep in the playa, usually boggy from winter rains, to evade coyotes and other predators. By day, they head for neighboring cornfields. Their morning take-off, generally 15 minutes before sunrise, is legendary. Ten to twenty thousand birds lift off in waves with an exciting cacophony of chattering, rattling and cooing. Observers swoon and describe this poetry in motion as one of nature's magical moments that's exciting to hear and spellbinding to watch.

The sandhill cranes aren't the only bird show around during the winter. Snow geese (p.156 bottom) intermix with the cranes in their roosting area. The playa also gets rife with raptors, attracting about 15 different species; and it becomes one of the best spots, nationally, for winter sparrows (about 20 different species). You may also spot javelina, mule deer, coyote and bobcat. One thing for sure about this beach, it's more than just wintertime fun; it's a winter wonderland of wildlife.

*P*retty, peaceful, and packed with wildlife, Roper Lake State Park presents a most unusual feature—permanent water—in the desert. The lake sings, chirps, croaks, and squawks with waterfowl, waterbirds, and songbirds. Especially during the spring and fall when many species pass through on the way to and from Central America. The year-round avian residents share their space, and sometimes flirt, with their human visitors.

The lake's lush vegetation, clean water, abundant supply of tasty fish and insects, an up-close backdrop of Mount Graham, and lots of wading and nesting spots might have something to do with the birds' preference for the lake. But just maybe the sophisticated, more worldly birds know Safford, located only 10 minutes north, has some of the best Mexican restaurants in the world. People aren't the only beings that like to be around good food.

Beyond birding, the park is full of ways for a family to have fun. Take a walk around the lake to view waterfowl; take a swim, put-in a kayak, or try sailboarding; explore the park's five-miles of hiking trails and maybe catch sight of wildlife like javelina, ringtails, and raptors; sit and soak in the stone-lined hot springs that

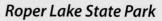

Roper Lake State Park

(928-428-6760) 101 E. Roper Lake Road, Safford

From US 70 go south on US 191about 5 miles to the signed turnoff

hover just-below body temperature; camp or rent a cabin for the night.

Though on the diminutive side, you'd never guess Roper Lake produces lunker fish. Arizona Department of Game & Fish stocks the lake with largemouth bass, catfish, crappies and trout. So throw in a line and get ready to snag 10- to 15-pound catfish or 11-plus pound bass. Then head for the park's grassy picnic area, called The Island, to grill the fish or feast on your favorite food. On Senior Salsa's advice, just don't forget to bring the salsa.

Top: Mt. Graham rises in the distance above the placid waters of Roper Lake. Above, right: Great egret skims the surface of Roper Lake; Below: Kayaker pauses momentarily as a flock of ducks makes a landing on Roper Lake.

Aravaipa Canyon Wilderness
Bureau of Land Management - Safford Field Office
928-348-4400 www.az.blm.gov

Drive west on US 70 to the signed turnoff for Aravaipa Canyon (between mileposts 113 and 114) and turn left (south). Drive about 32 miles to the town of Klondyke, then continue on the Aravaipa Road about 8.5 miles to the parking area. (The BLM advises a high clearance vehicle).

Hiking information: *The length of the canyon is 13.5 miles one-way. Length of stay is up to three days/ two nights. Most hikers average one-mile per hour. Permits required from the BLM.*

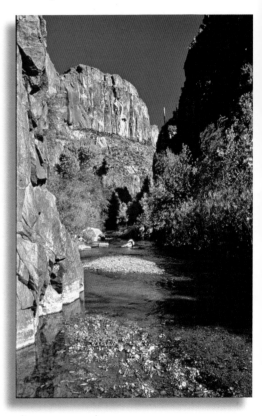

With major rivers flowing through its valleys, hot springs gurgling beneath its earth and water cascading down its mountains, it's not surprising to learn Arizona's Salsa Trail has yet another significant source of water. This one, Aravaipa Creek, has created an extraordinary environment in the Aravaipa Canyon Wilderness – one of the most biologically diverse areas in the state.

Located in the wild and remote Galiuro Mountains southwest of Safford, Aravaipa Creek flows past striking volcanic geology containing a meld of buff- and wine-colored peaks and cliffs rising 1,000 feet. A riparian forest of willow, Arizona walnut, Arizona sycamore, velvet ash and cottonwood trees grow along the year-round waters. The desert and its prickly appointments lie just beyond this streamside forest with stands of saguaro cactus crowding canyon slopes.

This desert stream draws almost four dozen mammals, from rodents to black bears, that scamper, pick and plod through the canyon. Wildlife events can range from a surprise moment with bighorn sheep clattering up ruddy rhyolite canyon walls, to entertaining thumps of a clan of coatimundis dropping from trees and scurrying away with their monkey tails proudly standing on end, to the poetry of a zone-tailed hawk dropping one of its white-banded tail feather onto the clear waters tinged with emerald reflections of streamside trees. More than a dozen species of bats keep busy through the night.

Aravaipa Canyon presents a true wilderness experience. No signs appear in the wilderness, nor do any maintained trails. Only beaten paths wind through the riparian habitat and splash back and forth across the creek. Often the creek becomes the trail, so wear footgear you can get wet.

Above: *the "Narrows" of Aravaipa Creek,* **Opposite Page:** *Above (1) gray fox in an alcove of the Red Knolls and* **Below:** *(2) overview Red Knolls, (3) Author in amphitheater of Red Knolls*

From Safford, go west on US 70 almost to milepost 312 and turn left (south) onto Red Knolls Road; drive about a half-mile to the knolls. High clearance vehicle is needed to explore the south end of the knolls. A spokesperson for the Bureau of Land Management advises the Red Knolls may not be safe to climb upon in spots.

*Without the sound of a hammer
or the touch of human hands
A veritable fortress in Arizona stands…*
from Red Knolls by Ruth Mary Fox

Once the accumulated sediment at the bottom of an ancient seabed, the Red Knolls rise Bryce-like from the desert floor in a most majestic manner. The Knolls' elegance comes from several amphitheaters etched with flutes, turrets, nooks and hoodoo columns topped with caps. Eastern Arizona College performed the Red Knolls Pageant from 1927 to 1935 in an amphitheater of the Red Knolls. The first production, the operetta *Lela Walla*, drew 1,500 people.

The Red Knolls carry a colorful history. Mormon poetess Ruth May Fox suggested in a poem she wrote about the curious formation that it was haunted by a supernatural power. Native peoples rendezvoused in the formations in centuries past. Cowboys used the natural amphitheaters to round up cattle. Rustlers used to hide out in the Red Knolls. Some corralled their clutch of stolen horses in the niches of the Knolls. Some, local legends say, buried their booty and never came back to get it.

Karen and Travis (and their dog, Murphy) from Safford hid a geocache among the Knolls called The Bottom of the Ocean memorializing the Knolls' genesis. The high-tech treasure hunt brought Team Bugman geocachers Bobby Martin and Marilyn Winker from Benson. Team Bugman not only found the cache that often eludes other geocachers, they saw a grey fox lounging in one of the Knolls' nooks.

Karen and Travis not only put the Red Knolls on the geocache map, they got married there. The reason? The Red Knolls once harbored a large colony of bats. Karen reported they have found three different species of bats. "Some people have doves at their wedding," Karen said. "We had bats." Bats, foxes, fossils, maybe even a little lost loot or at least a geocache. You never know what you'll find in this ancient anomaly.

Along the Salsa Trail - Destinations

Gila Box Riparian National Conservation Area
Bureau of Land Management Safford Field Office
928-348-4400; www.az.blm.gov

To reach the west side from Safford: *Go 5 miles east on US 70 to Solomon; turn left (north) onto Sanchez Road and follow the road to the end of the pavement; continue on the graded dirt road and follow the signs to Bonita Creek and the lower end of the Gila Box.*

To reach the east side from Safford: *Go 10 miles east on US 70 to its junction with US 191 and turn left (north); go 29 miles to milepost 160 and turn left (west) onto the signed Black Hills Back Country Byway; follow the road 4 miles to the conservation area. Contact the Bureau of Land Management or Graham County Chamber of Commerce for a map of the area.*

Like all perennial water sources, the Gila Box Riparian National Conservation Area has seen a lot of action through the eons. Yet this desert oasis darling has managed to keep its beauty and wild character intact. The area's riparian forest makes it a distinct and special place, special enough to have been considered for wilderness and national park status.

The Gila Box contains portions of the four waterways that flow around remote and rugged Turtle Mountain – the Gila River, its confluence with the San Francisco River, the lower end of Eagle Creek and Bonita Creek. All these waterways flow year-round, making them a place of choice for ancient and old-time homesteaders.

For centuries, the waterways of the Gila Box Riparian National Conservation Area have had an ebb and flow of humanity living along its banks, starting with prehistoric peoples, including Mogollon, Puebloan and Salado cultures. The Western Apaches set up rancherias along Bonita Creek where they tended cattle and raised crops. Mountain men explored and trapped along the waterways. Mexican, Chinese and European homesteaders raised cattle and goats and tended small farms and fruit orchards. In the 1920s, Bonita Creek's banks buzzed with humanity and accommodated small plots about a half-mile apart. Some historic homesteads, such as Old Lady Gay's cabin, remain.

The Gila Box takes its name from the high-walled canyon section of the Gila River that flows through the area. The Gila's flow gets substantial enough for kayak trips and rambunctious enough for whitewater rafting during snowmelt. The river courses through mesquite woodlands and galleries of cottonwoods, past sandy beaches and buff-colored cliffs. Arizona's first designated water trail, the Gila River Trail, travels on part of this segment of the Gila River.

More than 200 species of birds have been sighted throughout the Gila Box. Zone-tailed hawks nest in creekside cottonwood trees, green or belted king-fishers chatter on low-level flights above the water and neotropical birds drop in during migrations.

Bonita Creek - Cooled by a cocoon of sycamore, cottonwood and willow trees that coax an impressive list of avian and animal life to its side, Bonita Creek has become a wildlife sanctuary. All through the night, beavers sound off with the ker-plunk-splash of their bodies diving underwater for protection against the night moves of predators. Black bears grub along the creek banks and wild canine family members cruise its course. Bighorn sheep climb craggy canyon cliffs.

As wild as the Gila Box gets, the area exudes a soothing atmosphere for those who travel its backroads. Take the graded roads through a Lower Sonoran Desert landscape to Bonita Creek. Beyond the creek, the roads take a wilder mien and require high clearance and 4-wheel drive. The calm the countryside conveys seems an unusual characteristic for such a rough-and-tumble land once full of raucous times and personalities. But areas rich in culture often radiate a soothing coziness such as this, especially now that nature has the last say.

Farmers and merchants in the mid-1870s pieced together the Safford-Morenci Trail to pack their goods to the mining country. The ragtag route faded from memory for a time once automobiles came on the scene. Generally, the original route of the Safford-Morenci Trail headed northward from Safford into the Gila Mountains, writhed through Johnny Creek Canyon, waded Bonita Creek, climbed up colorful cliffs in Midnight Canyon, stood upon 6,800-foot-high Bellmeyer Saddle, dropped into South Smith Canyon, crossed Eagle Creek, then followed Gold Gulch into Morenci. Contact the Bureau of Land Management for more information on exploring this historical route.

Opposite page: *Views along Red Knoll Road,* **This page above:** *Autumn color frames Mt. Graham along the Gila River Water Trail (Arizona's first water trail) in early December.*

East of Eden
Thatcher, Bryce and Eden

I n 1878, the second generation of Mormon colonization started as Mormons moved into the Gila Valley. The venerable Mormon apostle, Erastus Snow, came by way of Reno Mountain Road through a rocky canyon in the Pinal Mountains, which he described as "a terrible place, almost impassable, the dread of all who travel this way." However, Mormon settlers soon followed and town sites appeared, first at Pima in 1879 and then Thatcher and Bryce.

Irrigation canal along Safford Bryce Road

The Mormon settlers sent an expedition to explore the "Valley of the Gila." The small group searched for the best place to dig an irrigation ditch. The group's chronicler, Hyrum Weech, wrote: "We traveled from one end of the valley to the other on both sides of the river, looking for the best place to take out a ditch, because we had very little means and could not go to large expense. This (near the location of Smithville, later known as Pima) seemed to be about the easiest place on the river to take out water, so we decided on making the location here."

Subsisting mainly on beans and bread, the Mormon settlers built the canal and eventually developed the land into high-ly productive farms. Pima, its neighboring communities of Thatcher, Bryce and Duncan still remain heavily Mormon.

Barn along Safford Bryce Road

Heading west of Safford on US 70, you can tour several of these Mormon towns. "Thatcher," wrote the Graham County Bulletin in 1895, "is the most beautiful town in the valley; its location is superb and its soil is rich. The houses are mostly of brick and some of the handsomest residences are found here including the President Layton home, the Bishop Claridge home and the Joe Layton home."

The historic Mormon community named for LDS Apostle Moses Thatcher keeps its cultural propensity for history and lineage alive. The little town has several historic buildings located on Church Street between 1st and College avenues that range from old and interesting to historic. Pick up a map at the Graham County Chamber of Commerce to guide you along.

For more Mormon heritage and a countrified scenic drive, go north on 8th Avenue (from US 70 in Saf-

Silo converted to offices

Desert scene along Hot Springs Road

ford) across the Gila River to Safford Bryce Road. Turn east (left) and follow the road past cotton farms, old buildings, irrigation canals and picturesque sights. Look for an unusual silo on the north side of the road.

The road bends into Bryce-Eden Road and passes the community of Bryce. Named for Ebenezer Bryce, for whom Bryce Canyon National Park was named, Arizona's Salsa Trail's Bryce is where the Mormon leader lived later in life. Check out the Bryce Cemetery on the north side of the road. The cemetery has the graves of the founding Mormon pioneers, some of whom served in the Civil War.

Continuing west, you come to the town of Eden. Look for the Eden Store, Eden Post Office and Merryland social hall.

For a little adventure, turn right onto Hot Springs Road, which takes you to the outskirts of town past farms and ranches. After about 9.5 miles, turn left (south) and go about 7.3 miles to US 70. A left turn will bring you back to Safford.

Our Lady of Guadalupe Shrine

Solomon
About 5 miles east of Safford off US 70

Solomon, the little town with a long list of former names, hardly lets on about the important place in Gila Valley history it played. The town, named for Isadore Solomon, originally went by the name of Pueblo Viejo, then Munson (some sources say Munsonville), Solomonsville and Solomonville.

When Isadore Solomon and his wife, Anna, arrived in Pueblo Viejo in the middle of a steamy August night in 1876, mostly Hispanic farmers lived in the highly fertile valley. Ancestral Puebloans originally built the town site, which was named for their ruins. The Arizona Territorial Governor A.P.K. Safford, for whom Safford was named, declared the ruins "one of the largest as well as the finest cities of the time."

After a few months of camp-style living, which Anna said she didn't mind save

Our Lady of Guadalupe Shrine, the historic church dates from 1878

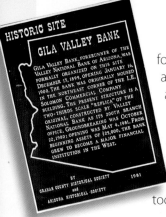

for the green pools of water, which probably caused fever and chills for a couple years, the Solomons bought land and started an impressive life in the Gila Valley. The town's name changed to Solomonville (after incorrectly named Solomonsville by the post office) and the town became the county seat in 1883 for 35 years until, Solomon writes, "they cut up that county and took the richest part to Clifton and made the county of Greenlee. What was left they took back to Safford where the county seat is now."

Isadore Solomon started the Gila Valley Bank, located at 2100 S. Bowie Avenue. The bank's first bookkeeper, Mary Woodman, had a hand in starting the bank's maiden branch in Clifton when she helped transport $800 to it. Mary carried $600 of silver dollars in cloth bags under her full, flouncy skirt, and three male escorts carried $200 in gold certificates to appease thieves in case they were robbed. They made the trip uneventfully.

The Solomons sold their store and hotel around 1919 and moved to Los Angeles. The town never was the same after the Solomons left and petered out after a number of droughts. In 1922, Gila Valley Bank merged with Phoenix's Valley National Bank. Now the University of Arizona owns the building.

Round Mountain Rockhound Area
Fire Agate Treasures

Go east on US 70 past Duncan, into New Mexico, to the turn-off for Lazy B Ranch between mileposts 5 and 6; turn right and go 7 miles to a fork and veer left; go about 5 miles to the rockhound area; a 5-mile-long (high clearance required) loop road travels around Round Mountain.

Arizona's Salsa Trail may not have caches of the planet's more glamorous gemstones of diamonds, rubies and opals, but it does have pockets of glittering crystals, geodes and fire agates. The big draw at Round Mountain, located near the Lazy B Ranch where U.S. Supreme Court Justice Sandra J. O'Connor grew up, is the semi-precious fire agate.

Round Mountain, a hill rising in the flatlands by the Peloncillo Mountains, has one of the best deposits of fire agates in the world. Scattered among an impressive cover of chalcedony, you can make some great finds of unique quartz, chalcedony in a variety of shapes and sizes and the rare fire agate.

"The opaline colors set the fire agates apart," said Bureau of Land Management Safford Field Office geologist, Larry Thrasher. "The only other mineral that iridescences is opal."

Old timers called fire agates cinnamon opal. In the raw, fire agates look like bubbly globs colored with orange to blood-red hues. The green and blue colors, which occur inside the rock, are produced by iron oxide.

"You have to cut and polish the stone to make it gem quality," Larry said. "Collectors learn what to look for."

Sometimes you can get a hint of the fire inside by wetting a likely stone and holding it up to the sun. When polished, the stone (which measures a hardness of 7 on the Mohs scale) becomes mesmerizing as burning embers – much like

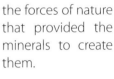

the forces of nature that provided the minerals to create them.

Most all of the mountain ranges around Arizona's Salsa Trail formed from volcanic activity. During eruption, lava and gases belched from the earth. Pockets of gas formed in the lava and when the molten substance cooled, the lava hardened and the gases escaped leaving a hollow chamber called a vesicle. Mineralization happened when the vesicle filled with water carrying silica, often from the lava itself, percolating down into the rock. Over time, the vesicles filled with silica and formed chalcedony and crystalline quartz. Fire agates formed when iron oxide mixed with the silica, growing layers of chalcedony with layers of ruddy iron oxide.

"The rock hounding area is a real adventure," said Larry, "and you get neat little rocks to show for it."

Olney House B&B

(928-428-5118) 1104 S. Central Avenue, Safford • olneyhouse.com

"It's just a big old comfortable house with a lot of history," said Chris Gibbs, owner and innkeeper of the Olney House Bed & Breakfast. "We've lived in Europe too long not to know a bed and breakfast is basically a stay in someone's home, not a luxury hotel. We tell people who stay more than a day to think of it as their home."

Not your typical fluffy Victorian, the big, rambling but cozy, Olney House stays relatively true to its period with furnishings patterned after how a rich family would have lived from George III through Edwardian periods (late 1700s to mid-1900s). Chris' wife, Deborah, has taken her time searching for the right furniture and fabrics, sometimes finding spot-on matches by accident. The result has produced harmonious and graceful interiors.

Built in 1890 for Sheriff George A. Olney and listed on the National Registry of Historic Buildings, the home is one of the Southwest's finest examples of Western Colonial Revival architecture. It's also a veritable museum of antiques and collectables that Chris and Deborah picked up from places they've lived and visited around the world.

"Most were purchased in England," Chris said. "We had a lot of fun collecting them. We thought we'd open an antique store, but everything we bought, we wanted to keep."

The engaging host loves to share things with people – especially kids, who generally have no idea what half the items in the dining room might have been used for.

Smiling mischievously, Chris pointed to two metal items at either side of a shelf on the dining room wall. "Do you know what these are? They're toasters for a wood-burning stove. People usually never correctly guess." Next, he pointed to a print of the Titantic Steamship that he acquired in London and signed by Michel Navratil, the last male survivor of the 1912 tragedy.

The old curiosities make for interesting conversation pieces. But not as interesting as one Chris and Deborah found right inside the home. During restoration of a room, they found a $50,000 check from Sheriff Olney to his son.

"It was a live check," Chris said. "I turned to Deborah and suggested we could contact the bank."

Ever the collectors, the Gibbs kept the check.

David A. James

Simpson Hotel in Duncan
(928-359-3590) 116 Main Street, Duncan • simpsonhotel.com

When Deborah Mendelsohn bought the old Simpson Hotel it was a "pretty dilapidated building." She didn't get but halfway up the stairs when knew she had to buy the historic building.

"It reminded me of the old buildings in my hometown of Boston," Mendelsohn recalled. "It was the whole Eastern Seaboard effect."

She restored the 1914 building back to its attractive character and made it a "green" hotel. Each room has period interiors updated only by luxurious beds and central heat to make them even more comfy-womfy. She also includes a hearty-size breakfast that's healthy for you.

"Other than that," Mendelsohn said, "you will find the Simpson to be much as it might have been a century ago, with no televisions or other modern effects in the rooms. However we do have wireless Internet that works throughout the building."

Across the street at the restaurant, Humble Pie, Pete Flood cooks up some of the best pizza in the Southwest. His credo, giving people a good product at a good price no matter how rural the town, backs up the boast. This may sound like a big statement, but how can you dispute someone who admits his calling in life is to make pizza, and a darn good pie at that? You'll understand after your first bite.

Down the street from the Simpson Hotel the visitor's center serves up coffee and espresso drinks. One newcomer has started plans to plant a vineyard and open a gourmet bistro.

All this might sound a little extravagant for the mostly salt-of-the-earth people that live in Duncan, population approximately 713. The town's mix of Mormon, Mexican, Arkansas pioneer and artisans like the rural setting with big skies that don't quit and a river that packs a scenic punch and draws enough birds to make a birder do a double take. But Duncan always did have entrepreneurial bones and residents with cheeky spirits. Like the late artist Hal Empie who had his studio in a drug store. The Art Gallery Drug had wall-to-wall carpet-

Along the Salsa Trail - Real Arizona

ing and piped-in music. The pharmacist sold his creative paintings and Kartoon Kards (published in Arizona Highways as early as 1938) while blending prescriptions and serving ice cream sodas. Often, he'd talk artistic techniques for hours. You can spot his paintings and stained glass window designs around town (as well as a collection of works in his namesake gallery in Tubac run by daughter Ann Groves).

The bottom line is: Duncan is the type of place where people let you be what you want to be. Duncan sees people from all walks of life pass through on its historic highway, US 70. They stop for a night or two, look around the town and fall for the town's charm. They come back to restore the old hotel, or open the pizza place or plant the vineyard. After all, it's probably their calling.

Opposite page: *above (1) Owner Deborah Mendelsohn, Below house cat, Frack.* **This page above:** *(1) Pete Flood's Humble Pie Pizza Parlour and his famous pizza, (2) Guest room at the Simpson Hotel, (3) A typical Simpson Hotel hearty breakfast.*

Potter Ranch Bed & Breakfast

(928-865-4847) Potter Ranch Road Clifton
(just off Frisco Road; about 1.8 miles from the bridge)

"There are gold mines all over these mountains," said June Palmer as she looked up at the towering canyon walls along the San Francisco River and pointed to a peak just across the road from her bed and breakfast. "The mine in that one built this home."

June's home, at first blush, looks recently built with a touch of old-time fancy. The unusual-looking home has a gingerbread quality to it, as if it were the setting for a fairy tale. When June described the home's history and how she revived it, the fairy tale turns into a dream come true.

"My grandfather, Del Potter, built the home," June said about the Moorish Mission Revival-style house with a wrap-around porch. "People called it a folly."

Del Potter – army colonel, Indian scout, deputy US Marshal, deputy sheriff, mining entrepreneur, self-taught and successful lawyer, founder and president of the Ocean-to-Ocean Highway Association and bona fide romantic – built the home in 1901. People called it "a folly" because of its location, right along the San Francisco River. Designed with ingenious features cutting-edge for the time, Del built a breakwater to protect the home and used the swift-flowing river water for electricity. Del planted 1,500 fruit trees and 300 ornamental trees, fragranced the porch with wisteria vines and used the river to irrigate the groves.

The mine that provided the money to build this dream estate, the Golden Ophir, was just one of about 600 patented mines Del discovered in the area. Del lived off the pockets of gold from his mining business. June was born on the Potter Ranch and remembers its Edenic opulence. She called Del, who always wore a suit and a Panama hat, a country gentleman.

Eden felt tremors when Del's wife, Lizzie died in 1917. Del and his sister, Olive, continued to live at the ranch, entertaining and living high on the hog until the Depression rocked Eden. With the mines playing out and money tightening, Del had to take out a loan to repair the roof. He added a stipulation to the contract stating if he defaulted, which he did, he and his immediate family could stay in the home.

the Salsa Trail - Real Arizona

Del died in 1942. Aunt Olive, proud but poor, lived in the house until she died in 1948. Phelps Dodge (now Freeport-MacMoRan Copper & Gold Inc.) eventually took over the property and leased it. The flood of 1983 delivered the final blow. What the flood did

not destroy, vandals did during the seven years the home stayed vacant.

"Bullet holes riddled the walls," June described the senseless acts of violence with sadness, "Windows were broken, doors destroyed or missing and the two fireplace mantels gone."

When June decided to restore the property, things started to fall into place. She sold her property in California, bought this home and most of the property (20 of the 60 acres washed away in floods) and began the process.

"I thought it was time to start, even if I didn't finish," June said. "The place was waiting for me. Plus, I could do my pastels and oils of landscapes. I learned to paint from my Aunt Olive."

June recalls the process, which started in 1981. She had to remove several feet of silt washed up from the river under the home. Though the 18-inch-thick adobe walls withstood the flood, the plaster interior walls melted from floodwaters. She replaced most of the windows herself. A friend gave her a fireplace mantel and she found one for the second fireplace at a flea market; both fit perfectly. June's dream came true when the home became livable in 1991.

"They say you can never go back," June remarked after recalling her labor of love, "but I did."

Opposite page: *above (1) owner June Palmer, (2) Col. Del Potter, (3) Kitty Potter Cosper (June's mother) (4) June Potter as a young girl.* **This page above:** *(1) Copper King Mountain with the Potter Ranch at the base (2) Pencil rendering of the Potter House, (3)* **below,** *the elegant Potter House dining room.*

Surrounded by cliffs rising like the fingers of a cupped hand in the Santa Teresa Mountains southwest of Safford, Black Rock Ranch makes a good place to give civilization the slip. Not much has changed on this historic piece of property since Hollis Holladay founded it in the 1890s. The area's demeanor lags decades behind the 21st century as if the mountains reside in a time warp where nature still rules and the men that frequent its slopes look the same as the cowboys who tried to tame it.

"The main thing about the ranch is its history," said Holladay's grandson, Newell Dryden, "and it's real. This ranch is not themed. It's not a dude ranch. It's the real thing."

Hollis, the first game warden in the Eastern Arizona Territory, deputy sheriff and Pima town marshal, lived there with his wife, Ina. He and Ina homesteaded the area, eventually gaining title, right next to its namesake, Black Rock, which vaults skyward from the high desert floor. Now third-generation Newell and Bunny Dryden own the ranch and open it to corporate and family retreats.

Every building in the ranch compound is full of antique and collectible ranching relics and old clothes family cowboys used though the years. The comforting smell from the old wood of the main house invites guests to sit down and stay a spell. Or maybe it's the smell of something cooking on the century-old wood-burning stove. The sounds of birds and glimpses of wildlife keep guests rocking on the front porch well past breakfast. This is a retreat, after all, generally from reality, as most people know it.

The area always did make a good retreat, more often for the wild and woolly, however, than the corporate folks and families who come here these days. The Santa Teresas' secluded outback provided a natural haven for people who wanted to disappear, particularly outlaws and anyone on the lam.

Along the Salsa Trail - Real Arizona

174

Newell's grandfather got a chance to meet many of these fugitives while he patrolled the mountains. Sometimes Holladay would get supplies for them when they'd provide lists and money. Newell's mom and aunt used to bring biscuits and jam to Old Man Fisher, wanted for shooting a man in Texas, then stay and listen as Fisher played the fiddle and feasted on the homemade goodies.

The Black Rock Ranch folk still have people feasting on homemade goodies. Bunny, chief cook and cowboy poetess, cooks up a legendary pot of beans and stew. This would be after the homemade biscuits and gravy for breakfast, which comes after her recital of a poem to greet the morning. Newell and sons have guests learning the cowboy trade of roping and then watching a branding, culling, vaccinating and sorting.

This far-from-ordinary ranch in this far-from-ordinary place has gotten some far-from-ordinary comments. "Wow," exclaims one written in the guestbook; "Amazing Place," describes another; "Seventh Wonder of the World," claims another; and then: "Bunny for President." Bunny for president? Yup, this is no ordinary place.

Opposite page: *Above, Newell Dryden, below: Black Rock ranch is located in the Santa Teresa Mountains,* **This page, above:** *Cowboy Poet Bunny Dryden,* **middle:** *Jess the mule, a world class cutter discussing the BLM,* **below:** *Interior of meeting room at Black Rock Ranch*

When you hear the word "cowboy"
What is it that you see,
A massive guy in Western duds
Or someone small like me?

It's come to stand for one who rides
And gives honor to a brand
But doesn't necessarily
Have to be a man.

When I hear the word "Cowboy"
The image it is clear.
It stands for guys and gals alike;
A word that I hold dear.

To be a "Cowboy" means much more
Than jeans and a cowboy hat,
A pair of gloves, red bandana,
Spurs and a lariat.

It stands for morals, trust and worth,
"Cowboy" stands for pride …
There ain't no gender in "Cowboy",
It's who you are inside.

From Cow Trails & Pony Tales
By Bunny Dryden, A Rancher's Wife (who stands all of
about five feet, give or take an inch or two)

. . . Books by Christine Maxa

- *Arizona: An Explorer's Guide*
  Countryman Press - W.W. Norton, New York & London

- *Arizona's Salsa Trail - A Foodies Guide to Culinary Tourism*
  Jamax Publishers Press, Kirkland, Arizona USA

- *Arizona's Best Wildflower Hikes - The Desert (2nd Edition)*
  Jamax Publishers Press, Kirkland, Arizona USA

- *Wickenburg - Hispanic Pioneer Families*
  Jamax Publishers Press, Kirkland, Arizona USA

- *Cycling Arizona - The Statewide Road Biking Guide*
  Westcliffe Publishers Englwood, Colorado USA

- *Wickenburg Adventures*
  Jamax Publishers Press, Kirkland, Arizona USA

- *Arizona's Best Wildflower Hikes - The High Country*
  Jamax Publishers Press, Kirkland, Arizona USA

- *Arizona's Best Autumn Color*
  Jamax Publishers Press, Kirkland, Arizona USA

- *Hiking Arizona*
  Human Kinetics - USA, Canada, United Kingdom